An
INCOMPLETE
and
INACCURATE
History of Sport

Also by Kenny Mayne

Nothing

An
INCOMPLETE
and
INACCURATE
History of Sport

Kenny Mayne

Crown Publishers
New York

The "Forward" by Larry Bird is printed by permission of Larry Bird®. Copyright © 2008 by Larry Bird.

Photograph and illustration credits:
xv: Ichiro: Scott Clarke; xvi: Immaculate Reception: Riley Mayne; xvii: explanation of Immaculate Reception: Riley Mayne; xix: perfect game: Annie Mayne; xx: explanation of perfect game: Annie Mayne; 23: Dennis Johnson and Gus Williams: Seattle SuperSonics; 26: Untitled: Riley Mayne; 28: pasta: istockphoto.com; 43: *In America*: © 2003 Twentieth Century Fox Film Corporation; 60: drawings of their father: Riley and Annie Mayne; 65: *Dancing with the Stars*: © ABC (American Broadcasting Companies, Inc.); 78: depictions of *Dancing with the Stars*: Riley and Annie Mayne; 80: Football: Riley Mayne; 81: Randy Moss: Scott Clarke; 89: electric tackle football: Scott Clarke; 98: bass fishing: ESPN; 119: horse racing: Santa Anita; 123: Longacres: David Grant Best; 128: downhill track: Santa Anita; 135: Starbucks: Annie Mayne; 146: Kenny playing for UNLV: UNLV; 167: Brett Favre: Scott Clarke; 168: Tom Brady: Scott Clarke; 176: NFL peekaboo: Scott Clarke; 184: Randall Cunningham: Rusty Kennedy; 187: Randall Cunningham: Riley Mayne; 194: tetherball illustrations: Riley and Annie Mayne; 199: Montana and Walsh: Michael Zagaris; 200: Wiffle ball: Kenny Mayne; 203: Wiffle ball: Riley Mayne; 218: Ken Griffey, Jr.: KWPX TV; 220: The Connor: Riley Mayne; 221: Connor Mayne: Kenny Mayne; 221: Kenny's dad: Kenny Mayne; 229: Modern Art: Riley and Annie Mayne.

Published in the United States by Crown Publishers, an imprint of the Crown Publishing Group, a division of Random House, Inc., New York.
www.crownpublishing.com

Crown is a trademark and the Crown colophon is a registered trademark of Random House, Inc.

The chapter titled "Wiffle Ball: Haunted by Ghost Runners" is a reprint of an ESPN.com story written in September 2001, with permission of ESPN.

Library of Congress Cataloging-in-Publication Data

Mayne, Kenny.
An incomplete and inaccurate history of sport / Kenny Mayne.—1st ed.
p. cm.
Includes index.
1. Sports—Humor. I. Title.
PN6231.S65M34 2007
818'.602—dc22 2007040946

ISBN 978-0-307-39615-0

Printed in the United States of America

Design by Level C

10 9 8 7 6 5 4 3 2 1

First Edition

For Laura,
the one I'm always seeking to impress

Contents

Foreword

It's probably more powerful to have some kind of famous person write the foreword to your book.

Let this be the first of many disappointments as you read more.

To begin with, the book isn't really *complete*. Lots of sports are never mentioned at all.

In fact, there is every chance you can blow through the book while standing at a Barnes & Noble, Borders, Books-A-Million, Hastings, Chapters (for those of you in Canada), or an independent bookseller of your choice while waiting for your wife, girlfriend, mistress, or the opposite if you are female. (Let the record show I like females. Females are good readers.) Anyway, you should be able to read this thing in roughly the same amount of time it takes that person you are waiting for to finish arguing with the cashier as to whether the "10% off" sticker is in addition to, or exclusive of, the discount associated with his or her book club membership.

If you go this route, please don't damage the cover, as it is intended to be displayed as a coffee-table book. Or at least used as a coaster.

As for ongoing disappointments, in addition to not being complete, the book is not particularly *accurate*. If this were a history book, then Ken Burns would have been involved and it would have taken four or five years to produce. I wrote this thing in four or five hours, and that time would have been reduced a great deal had my daughters not kept interrupting me to play indoor tackle football. They know ten different pass routes, all off of audible calls at the line of scrimmage, which is over by the television set.

While being neither complete nor historically accurate, my book *is* about sports. At times.

I get to cover sports for a living. This is ridiculous. Other people have real jobs. They make things. They sell stuff. They put out fires. I just watch sports. Then I make up stories about the sports I watch.

In this effort, if you can call it that, I've tried to be honest, except in those cases where making something up helped finish a paragraph. I won't say writing the book was easy, but it wasn't exactly coal mining either.

The inspiration for this book came from my literary agent, Michael Murphy. He saw me inside his television and was moved to send me countless e-mails encouraging me to write a book. He probably just wanted to make money, but he said all the right things. Perhaps he'll stop sending me e-mails now.

I've never even met the guy. He could be a war criminal for all I know. If so, I probably don't have to give him any money. He should be hanged. The bastard.

My other inspiration was the Jon Stewart book on democracy. I think it was called *Democracy* or maybe it was called *An Incomplete and Inaccurate History of Democracy.* (Publisher's note: It was called *America (The Book).*) Anyway, it was funny.

I hope I have done for sports what Jon Stewart did for democracy. Since his book came out, our great nation has not been taken over by Communists. Not yet.

As I write, one thought keeps going through my head: "If I exclude a glossary or whatever that section is that comes at the end of some books, I can be done writing sooner." (Publisher's note: That thing is called an index.)

At the same time, I love words. I love writing. Why else would I have written this coaster?

I have decided to cut the price by 75 percent. Under twelve dollars seems like a fair price, way better than forty-eight dollars.

And I don't think Canadians should have to pay extra. Why does the book industry hate Canada? Why don't books have little stickers that penalize instead Mexicans or Hondurans? (Publisher's note: Author has no say in pricing of the book.)

This book is dedicated to Canadians. I'm going to write my first chapter on hockey.

Enjoy your coaster.

Backwords

I do believe this is the first *backwords* in publishing history. I didn't find another one in my exhaustive research at a local bookstore. Then again, my daughters Riley and Annie made me stop when we were knee-deep in the transportation section.

This is so revolutionary it is holding up the opening chapter on ice hockey, dedicated to all those Canadian people, the targets of an oppressive book industry.

Seems like a good time for a photograph now.

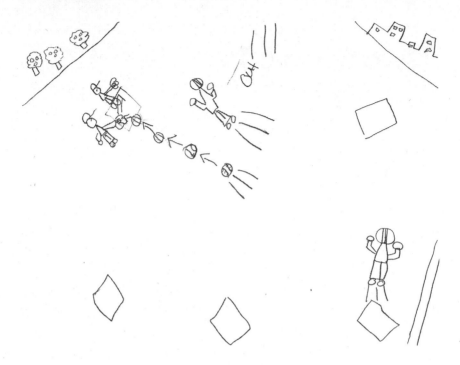

Here is my daughter Riley's illustration of the Immaculate
Reception. You know, the famous play in which Franco Harris
caught the ball after it bounced off the ground and Pittsburgh beat
Oakland.

It would appear Riley was inspired to draw something of a hybrid illustration in which football and baseball converge but on a
day where not many players showed up. I don't know what Riley
was thinking. That is why I asked her to explain herself. Usually
when I ask her to explain herself it's because she has sprayed a full
can of Raid into the fireplace and our couch is in flames. This time
I just wanted to know why she drew a hybrid football-baseball
game with not enough players when you'd think after knowing me
for eight years or so we would have talked about Franco Harris at
least once.

Below is Riley's explanation. She earned five dollars for this. She
spent it on earrings at the mall. These are the fake pierced earrings

that squeeze onto her earlobes and dent them. She will have lost
them long before this gets printed, but at least we have the following:

Bing!! The ball hit off the bat. I ran as fast as I could
to first base. I had to make it!! I was running out of breath.
Would I stop? Would I go on? I was now running faster
than before. I was about to stop. My teammate was running
to second OUT they yelled did they mean me?..........
Nope I kept running I stoped breating I was about to touch first
when....,,,,

Forward

Larry Bird

I can't believe Kenny Mayne is trying to delay his hockey chapter by using another gimmick this early in the book. I was a *forward*, get it? He tried to tell me how funny it would be if a forward wrote a forward for him, some kind of lame literary inside joke playing off the fact books have *forewords*.

He also told me how I was his favorite forward of all time but little does he know I just ran into Karl Malone, Dennis Rodman, and Xavier McDaniel.

I think this is pretty stupid but I'll tell you what *is* funny. What's funny is the picture just below. Kenny asked his daughter Annie to draw up Don Larsen's perfect game, and she illustrated bowling.

Like her sister, Annie also wrote up a little paragraph trying to explain why her father had never sat her down to talk with her about Don Larsen's perfect game. What kind of parenting is that?

As I understand it, at the time Riley was spending her five bucks on the fake earrings, Annie was being forced to try on back-to-

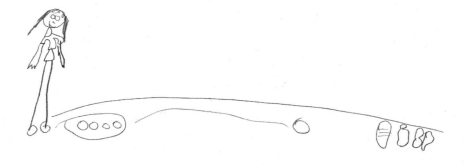

I think that you Know How When
your Bolling how When
you Nonk down all the Fings
the top sds PerFRCt game
so I dra Bolling

Perfect game

school clothes. No wonder she feels left out as the second child. Tell you what, I'll buy her the fake earrings if they're going to treat her that way. There's no way Malone was better than me. And I know I'm just a hick, but as far as contextual continuity goes, don't you think it would have made a whole lot more sense to run the ice hockey chapter just after the mention in the foreword about how Canadians have to pay extra money for books? That's how I would have done it.

An
INCOMPLETE
and
INACCURATE
History of Sport

Still by Kenny Mayne

Ice Hockey

Barry Melrose was one of the greatest coaches in the history of professional ice hockey.

Currently, he is the greatest professional ice hockey commentator in the history of professional ice hockey commentating.

And "O Canada" is a way better song than "The Star-Spangled Banner."

Some people reading this are thinking, "If you like Canada so much, why don't you just move there?" To those people I say, "Will you help me move?" and "Can I borrow your truck?"

Hockey was invented a long time ago by people who had nothing better to do when ponds would freeze.

The point of the game is to make a rubber disk go past a line at the front of a goal area. When that happens, a red lamp is lighted and the people watching punch each other on the arm and spill beer. That's unless the red lamp is lighted by the visiting team, in which case the people just spill beer.

In ice hockey players often get into fights. It is rare in sport (see also the boxing chapter I wrote and the cockfighting chapter I did not) that the officials in charge stand back and allow fights to continue. In ice hockey, however, fighting is given tacit approval by the officials.

"Tacit" is the fanciest word I've used so far and it contains just four or five letters.

If I remember correctly, ice hockey uses about six players on each side. Teams have more players than that—otherwise who would the six players sit next to on the plane? The players who aren't on the ice tap their hockey sticks on the floor to encourage players who are on the ice. The players on the floor aren't encouraged by this, because they cannot see or hear the sticks being tapped on the floor, due to the fact somebody on the other team has them in a headlock or their faces are being smashed into the protective glass surrounding the rink.

Wayne Gretzky is arguably the greatest ice hockey player ever. He was better at being a player than Melrose was at being a coach or is at being a commentator. I mentioned Melrose earlier because he's a good guy who one time handled an entire three-minute-long ice hockey highlight for me when I had to fill in on the *NHL 2Night* on ESPN2 when Bill Pidto was ill. The *NHL 2Night* highlight lad had delivered me a shot sheet (the notes written up to match the highlight video) for a thirty-second highlight, but then they instead rolled the three-minute version. I said to Barry, "You've always wanted to call a hockey highlight by yourself, right?" Then I walked away. Barry nailed the highlight without any notes in the same way I can make toast without a recipe. But back to Gretzky, who has never done anything for me.

The fact I'm calling him arguably the greatest ice hockey player ever when he's never read a hockey highlight for me says something. It says I'm probably minimizing his greatness by inserting "arguably" when his very nickname was and is the Great One. I don't know if he makes his wife or children call him the Great One. I used to make my daughters call me Sire or Lord of All Nations. That was back when they believed I invented the sun. Way before fake earrings.

Of Wayne Gretzky, Barry Melrose is quoted as saying the following: "a unique person and athlete who comes along very, very seldom." The fact Melrose said "very" twice makes me think there won't be an ice hockey player called Another Great One for a very, very long time.

"O Canada" is a good song but I'm not moving to Canada, because I don't know very much about ice hockey.

Here is one relevant fact about ice hockey.

In 1997, Scotty Bowman became the first coach in the history of the four major American pro sports to win titles with three different franchises. Bowman won a record nine Stanley Cups, five with the Canadiens, three with the Red Wings, and one with the Penguins.

This book is making an excellent coaster.

Australian Rules Football

Australian Rules football is very popular in Australia, where many people know the rules.

Very few people know the rules to tipping.

Sure, there are those little slide rules one can purchase to cut down the time spent calculating just what the waiter or waitress deserves. I'm speaking instead of the larger question, the true rules of tipping—a great philosophical dilemma.

I knew a guy in college who was taught by his parents that one should tip *one dollar* no matter the total price of the meal. That family is the reason waiters spit in food.

We know by now that tips should be around 15 to 20 percent of the total bill. Is that before or after taxes? What if the food costs $100 but your date picks out a rare $2,500 bottle of wine? Should the waiter be tipped the 15 to 20 percent on the entire bill? If so, the tip would exceed the cost of the food. That better be good wine.

Also, should there be a second date?

I don't have to worry about that last scenario, because I'm married and rarely drink.

But I do face the issue of tipping because of the great amount of travel I incur.

"Incur" is a strange-looking word.

My grand-nephew (I'm that old or my niece had a baby that young) James once tipped his teacher a twenty-dollar bill. He thought she was doing a good job.

That was one of the rare occasions where a tip was refused. In many cases, the tip is built into the pricing, often disguised under other names. At fine hotels, room service is delivered with a high base price and an automatic tip. With the addition of "service and delivery" charges, I once had a cheeseburger, salad, and Coke (not Pepsi) for seventy-eight dollars in New York City. There was a price for the actual food, another for the fact that the food was delivered to the room, and still another for the fact that a hotel employee had to push an elevator button *and* knock on my hotel room door. In addition, the room-service waiter did indeed offer a full review of exactly what had occurred.

Waiter: We have the cheeseburger, salad, and Coke.
Me: Right.
Waiter: Will there be anything else?
Me: No. I think seventy-eight dollars is enough.

It's at this point the waiter typically lingers in the room, unfolding my cloth napkin, inquiring as to whether ice cubes will be necessary, and pointing out how the Yankees are doing either quite well or not so quite well. It is at this point the waiter is hoping I put pen to paper and add *Additional gratuity.*

I will do no such thing.

I'm all for hefty tipping when the waiter or waitress has been a great sport, particularly *inside a restaurant.*

Waiter: Will there be anything else?
Me (circling the preassigned total on the bill): No. I think an effective tip rate of 25 percent is fair given the fact that all you did was push an elevator button and knock on my door.
Waiter: I did also announce all the items that had been delivered. They were cheeseburger, salad, and Coke.
Me: I'll put the tray in the hall.

Housekeepers? They should be tipped even more often than teachers. And teachers should split their tips with janitors.

Housekeepers should be tipped except in those cases *where they already are being tipped.* Some hotels now insert an extra 10 percent fee on the bill for "general services." When I caught this once in upstate New York, it was explained to me that the money is for the bellmen, valets, and housekeepers. Those were the same people who gladly accepted fives and tens from me all week.

The automatic tipping charges act as protection for staff in the event the hotel is full of people who would also be capping all restaurant tips at one dollar no matter the price of the meal. Most people, however, actually tip a fair amount of money for a fair amount of work. What the institutionalized tipping does is create a standoff in what ought to be a friendly exchange of money for service.

You know, the free market.

Bellman: Will there be anything else?
Me: You mean like me handing you more money?
Bellman: Pardon me?
Me: How 'bout you, the valet guys, and the housekeepers all run up to the front desk. They are holding your tip money in escrow.

I feel like a jerk right now for not tipping that bellman, and this is just a book.

Instead, even with the knowledge that I'm getting hammered at checkout, I'll fork over fives and tens to bellmen, valet attendants, and housekeepers just so they don't talk about me when I leave.

The automatic tipping charge is like the Alternative Minimum Tax. It was invented to catch cheats, but it ends up hammering those who might have been honest in the first place.

Will there be anything else? Yes. There will be the guy at the fancy hotel who hands you a valet parking slip.

Guy at Hotel Who Hands Me Valet Parking Slip: Will there be anything else?

Me: This five dollars?

Guy at Hotel Who Handed Me Valet Parking Slip and Accepted Five Dollars: Thank you.

Next in line is Guy Who Takes Luggage out of Excessively Large Family Vehicle Purchased to Guard Family Against Damage Caused by Other Excessively Large Family Vehicles. That guy takes our luggage out of the back and moves it *just inside the door of the hotel.*

Guy Who Took Luggage out of the Back of Excessively Large Family Vehicle Purchased to Guard Family Against Damage Caused by Other Excessively Large Family Vehicles: Will there be anything else?

Me: This ten bucks?

Next comes Guy Who Pushes Luggage on a Cart to the Bell Stand Area.

Guy Who Pushed Luggage on a Cart to Bell Stand Area: Will there be anything else?

Me: This ten bucks?

Then comes Nice Lady at Counter Who Actually Gives Us Keys to Our Room but who is ineligible to accept tips even though she has also said, "Will there be anything else?"

Me: Change for a hundred?

Next comes the actual bellman, the fifth person we've encountered, but only the fourth eligible for a tip. He works way harder than the guy mentioned previously who was automatically tipped for pushing an elevator button and knocking on my door. In this case, he doesn't have to push the elevator button, because my daughters fought each other for thirty seconds for the right to be the one who got to touch a filthy elevator button, and he doesn't have to knock on the door, because we open it for him with the key, but still he does have to lift a bunch of luggage and the cart looks like the Clampetts have arrived because we always pack like we are moving away permanently, so yes, he worked pretty hard relatively speaking. He gets a nice tip for all that but mostly because he *gives us back* our luggage.

> **Guy Who Gives Us Back Our Luggage:** Will there be anything else?
> **Me:** This twenty?

We've gone through forty-five dollars and all we have to show for it is the repossession of our luggage. We order cheeseburgers.

Later we go to dinner, in an actual restaurant, and encounter Waitress Who Is Mean Until the Two-Minute Warning to Moment of Tip Declaration. Throughout the meal she was impatient with the kids. She acted like we'd requested that she swim the English Channel when another fork was needed because Annie had launched the first one across the room. She cited government regulations when a small substitution request was made. She never looked at my wife.

But when the Two-Minute Warning to Tip Declaration was silently sounded, the girl was all smiles. Suddenly she had cleavage. She talked about the weather. She patted one of the girls on the head.

After an hour of surliness, she's selling kindness. But we're not buying.

We've seen this act before. It's too late for her to spit in our food. All she can do is talk about us.

Words are cheap. And in this case, so are we. But in this case, it feels rich.

A dollar for her.

Here's a bunch of facts about Australian Rules football, but I had to go and use tackle football in distributing the facts, which will probably have all you Australian Rules football people upset.

Fact: Australian Rules football was established to keep cricket players fit during winter.

	Australian Rules Football	American Tackle Football
Field shape	oval	rectangular
Players per side	18	11
Length of game	4 quarters	4 quarters
6 points for	goal	touchdown
1 point for	behind	extra point

Badminton

L ots of people call badminton "bad-mitten."
Those people don't know what they are talking about.

In badminton, your father takes about three hours to set up a net because there are rocks under the grass where he is trying to jam the posts in.

In the meantime, you and your friends kill each other with jokes about how the thing you are supposed to hit over the net, if your dad ever gets it set up, is called a "shuttlecock."

You keep repeating "shuttlecock" over and over. Eventually, one of your friends laughs so hard he pees his pants and has to go home to change clothes.

Shuttlecock.

I just peed my pants and would have to go home to change my clothes except I'm already home.

We live on a hill in Connecticut and the front yard is slanted so severely there is no shot at playing badminton, even if I let my daughters say "shuttlecock." Plus my dad died in 2001 so there is no one around to set up the game.

Anyway, in badminton, once your dad has set up the net, you hit the shuttlecock back and forth over the net. If it hits the ground on your side your opponent gets one point.

I think the games are played to 15, but who cares? Badminton is not as cool as tackle football but you usually don't break your femur as often. Then again, I've never seen anyone play badminton with Lawrence Taylor.

Here is a relevant fact about badminton.

Badminton premiered as a full medal Olympic sport at the 1992 Games in Barcelona. My friend, Tom Farrey, who also has a book called *Game On,* went to those Games and said he saw a lot of topless women.

Baseball

Baseball players are among the most superstitious of all athletes. I don't really know if this is true, but it's been repeated so often I'm going with it. And there's no way I'm going to call anyone to find out. To do otherwise would insult the integrity of this book's title.

I do know, from personal experience, that every baseball manager or player I have ever seen avoids touching the white chalk foul line when coming on or off the field.

I don't really know why baseball coaches are called *managers*. I have never heard a player say to a manager, "How are you today, manager?" They might say, "How are you today, *boss*?" Or, "How are you today, *skipper*?"

As far as I care to know, in every other sport except tetherball, the highest-ranking person on or near the field of play is known as the head coach. That is true except in those cases in which the general manager or owner comes down to the field from the luxury suite to poke and prod the players they own. In baseball, general managers and owners don't have to worry about touching or not touching the white chalk foul line, because they usually stay back by the batting cage and talk about the players.

The players are also talking about the general manager and the owner. Mostly they are saying bad things about each other. Typically, the owner is a guy who has lots of money because his father or grandfather had lots of money. That's with the exception of the owners who made a bunch of money in the 1990s when everybody thought the Internet would be a big deal.

Boy, were people wrong about that one.

Anyway, whether rich via their grandfather or via the Internet, the owner and his general manager don't have to worry about the white chalk line that much. They have subordinates to touch or not touch it for them.

Everyone else is terrified of that white chalk foul line even though a ball that hits the line is called fair.

In 2001, at the Major League All-Star Weekend in Seattle, I stood with some ex–big league players and colleagues and we all joked about how ridiculous the superstition is regarding the white chalk foul line. There were many of us standing around doing this, far too many to chronicle the names right here. In front of all these people I stomped all over the white chalk foul line on the third-base side. Nothing happened.

The next day I played in the so-called Legends and Celebrities Softball Game. I'm guessing I was a legend. Midway through the game, I tried to bring back an Alvin Davis home run that was ten feet over my head. I sacrificed my body, leaping nearly three inches off the ground at the end of a full-speed run. I slammed into the aluminum fencing that was being held up by high school students so that it wouldn't collapse when somebody like me tried to run through it. I hit my head and thought I was going to die.

Howie Long, the famous tackle football player who is probably in the Hall of Fame, ran over to me and asked, "Are you okay?" I told Howie, "I am not well." He then laughed for ten minutes. Somehow I managed to continue in the game. It was only a minor concussion I would find out later. What's a minor concussion when Jessica Biel is on my team?

I caught a fly ball to end the game (Biel threw one pitch to get the save) but in doing so I injured my knee. I didn't exactly judge the ball well and made an inelegant catch, while my left knee was hyperextended. An MRI the next day revealed no tear, just a minor sprain.

The next morning I was drying my hair when unbeknownst to me my electric hair dryer caught fire. As I continued my important grooming, tiny pieces of molten plastic hair dryer were being blown onto my face, eyelids, and hair. I yanked the flaming hair dryer's electrical cord out of the wall and went about removing shards of plastic shrapnel from myself. The hotel staff was very concerned. Very concerned that I might sue. What's some molten plastic hair dryer affixed to your eyelid when Jessica Biel was on your team?

Counting it up now, in roughly thirty-six hours since I'd stomped all over the white chalk foul line at Safeco Field, I had suffered a concussion, nearly blown out my knee, and was half an inch from being blinded by flying melted plastic.

I still think the superstition is ridiculous. Baseball players and managers and even coaches, owners, and general managers should come out of the Dark Ages and be free of this mindless tradition.

I have never stepped on a white chalk foul line since.

Way back when the foul lines weren't marked quite so neatly, I tried the game of baseball.

Fred George's dad, Vern George, was the coach. He may have been the manager too. Fred George would later break my ankle in ninth-grade tackle football. His dad seemed intent on breaking my face.

Vern George would stand on the pitcher's mound while inept, underdeveloped ten-year-olds like me stood trembling about fifty feet away. I stood ready (ready?) at home plate to try to field sizzling grounders off the bat of Vern George. Mostly I tried to *defend* myself from the lasers offered me by this full-grown man who shaved, drove cars, and mowed the lawn. He placed us with the backstop directly behind us because if not, in my case, it would have been a long afternoon having to go chase every single one of the balls he belted toward me.

Somehow, I avoided serious injury and having Rawlings emblazoned on my face. But I did not avoid being sent down to the Lesser Little Leagues. The players who could catch some of Vern George's grounders were rewarded with a roster spot on the Majors team. Those who did not cover their face with their glove were put into Double A. Dorks like me were placed in whatever the league was called that accepted players who had to be placed in *any league*.

Back before the heavy pressure of full-scale tryouts and cuts there was the Really Lesser Little League.

This was T-ball. Pretty much anyone could hit the ball off a tee.

I struck out off a tee.

With my older sister, Leslie, and her boyfriend watching behind home plate's backstop, I strode to the tee, a seven-year-old full of no confidence. None at all. Cover of *Dork* magazine.

On the first swing, I dribbled one off the tee about eleven feet from home plate. The umpire ruled it a strike, as the ball had to make it to the pitcher's area to count as being in play. On the second attempt, I swung mightily and missed. I thought I heard my sister's boyfriend yell, "Swing lower!" My sister buried her face in shame into her boyfriend's coat. That, or she was sexually active at age twelve.

It came down to this. On my third swing I *broke the tee in half.*

I don't know if breaking the tee in half should have counted as a strike. I doubt the umpire did either.

Some occurrences are just too far-fetched to have been included in the rule book. Maybe because it would have taken someone's dad half an hour to grab tools out of the back of his pickup truck and repair the broken tee, a consensus decision was reached by all the parents in attendance. The umpire, the father-coaches (not yet called managers), and some moms who saw the dinner hour approaching all looked at each other with one of those glances that said, "*This kid really sucks* and he'll probably break another tee if we repair that one."

They called me out on strikes. They played another inning with someone's dad pitching. I probably struck out off someone's dad too.

My baseball career flourished after that. I never struck out off a tee again. I pitched a no-hitter against Brack's Parker Paint while proudly wearing the red and green colors of LakeCrest 7-Eleven. But still, I couldn't hit my way out of a paper bag.

My baseball career ended in ninth grade. Spring baseball was my return to athletics after snapping my ankle the previous fall in tackle football. That sounds like a pretty good excuse for hitting .050, doesn't it?

One for twenty. I think the one was an infield hit that could have been ruled an error.

I lost interest in baseball and devoted all my time to tackle football. There were no bats involved and I had plenty of bones left to break.

I remained a fan of baseball. So much so that one time my late friend Warren Thomas and I paid off a security guard and found ourselves watching the Seattle Mariners and the Oakland A's at Oakland Coliseum for two dollars each.

The best baseball memories were free and, as the commercial says, priceless.

In 1995, I watched in person at Yankee Stadium as New York took a 2–0 wild-card playoff lead against my hometown Mariners. Three games later, Ken Griffey Jr. (who might have broken Aaron's mark before Bonds if not for the injuries) was sliding into home, smiling, and the Mariners had taken down the Yankees.

But my best memory was not a provincial thing. It was the night Cal Ripken Jr. broke the seemingly unbreakable "iron man" record for consecutive games played. That night, September 6, 1995, Ripken played in his 2,131st straight game, en route to his standing record of 2,632 games. (Is this book loaded with stats, or what?) Anyway, sixteen years without missing a day of work.

I can't remember my dad ever missing a day of work either, but his streak of selling airline tickets and loading passengers onto planes for United in Seattle just never caught the public's attention.

My wife, Laura, and I were on our honeymoon the night Ripken set the mark. We drove from Connecticut to Maine. No real plan. Just drive north each night until we found a spot to sleep, then a repeat of that the next day.

One night we found ourselves in a small cottage a few towns north of Portland, Maine. Our room was tiny, the black-and-white television maybe ten inches. And yet, it was one of the great TV experiences we'd ever witnessed, right there with the first walk on the moon, also seen in black and white.

The reception came in and out, the audio was hot then muted. But it was poetic.

Nothing funny happened.

Here is a relevant fact about baseball.

On June 14, 1996, Cal Ripken Jr. played in his 2,216th consecutive game, setting a new consecutive games "world record." The previous mark of 2,215 was held by third baseman Sachio Kinugasa, who played with the Hiroshima Carp in Japan's Central League. Off memory, I could have sworn Kinugasa had played in 2,214 games.

Basketball

Basketball is a sport in which I could not hit a jumper to save my life.

The best basketball played in my vicinity was in 1979. That's when the best three-guard offense ever, Gus Williams, (the late) Dennis Johnson, and Fred Brown helped take the Sonics to their one and only NBA title.

The greatest moment in the history of Seattle Sonic NBA titles came when *play was stopped.* It was the title series in the spring of '79. The Bullets (who would later be called Wizards, and by the way, Gus was nicknamed the Wizard) had called a time-out after a big Seattle run. The Sonics didn't take a long time in the huddle. After all, it wasn't their idea to call a time-out. They were doing fine.

As the Bullets continued to break chalk and devise a plan to stop the Sonics, the Seattle players came onto the court. Gus and D.J. ended up under the basket at one end. They grabbed the ball from one of the refs and started flipping little two-foot backhand shots into the hoop. They stood there laughing, eating up the moment. They owned the game and we owned the Bullets. (Fans of professional sports teams use the word "we" as though the entire town is part of one large high school. The use of "we" is seen most often when a team is on the verge of winning a league title. The use of "we" carries even more power when the league involved decides to call its championship a world championship even if it's really a championship only for teams located in North America.) (Portions of this will be repeated in the next chapter because I wrote some similar-sounding stuff a few months apart due to the fact that I have poor organizational skills and don't always plan ahead. Speaking of plan ahead, my mom once taught me a lesson about how to prepare for the future.

On a piece of paper she wrote out—P L A N   A H E A

I see her point now that I have two similar basketball chapters.)

Back when the Sonics weren't being world or even league champions, when they weren't even competing so swell in the old Pacific Division, their stage still seemed fairly large to a twelve-year-old. Times were different. Either that, or my parents were totally irresponsible. (Even though my mom was pretty big on Planning.) In those days our parents (my friends' included) would allow us to take a bus to downtown Seattle from fifteen miles to the south. The parents would rotate after-the-game pickup responsibilities.

My wife and I don't let our girls farther away from us than the brussels sprouts when we are standing by the asparagus. But in the early 1970s all parents smoked cigarettes and used their right arm for seat belts.

The Sonic games were great, I'm certain. Wilt Chamberlain could have been in town, for goodness sake. But the name we saw on the marquee was freedom.

We'd buy the cheapest ticket available, then spend the entire first quarter scouting for open space nearer the court. In fact, I cannot recall one detail of one play from any first quarter I witnessed.

By early second quarter, Shawn Doran, his brother Dennis, Lips (Danny Sargent), and I were five rows up at center court.

The halftime show wasn't much in those days. The Sonics had a giant stuffed animal named Wheedle (as in Space Needle, I suppose) who worked the crowd. They also brought out a fan to shoot for a Buick from half-court. We rarely stayed for the entirety of the show. Halftime was start time. Twelve-year-olds were free to use a playpen of unlimited potential. Tag, hide-and-seek, water spitting, just plain acting silly. Who knew what went on in the game during the third and fourth quarters? Who cared?

The crowning achievement of the night was to get a player to talk to you after the game. On the playgrounds we would hear the sad tale of Matt McCully in his attempt to bond with the great Oscar Robertson. Matt was *way* older than us. Four years older.

Back at our age he had an audience with the Big O in the corridor leading to the Milwaukee Bucks' bus.

Matt: Big O! Big O! Hi. My name is Matt. Matt McCully. I'm your biggest fan. I play point guard for Sacajawea Junior High School. I love the way you play. I try to set up the other guys like you. I love assists. I was just wondering—

Big O: Man, get the hell out of my face.

The story made its way to our generation of locker-room rats. It should have been a cautionary tale of how one cannot expect too much from these stars. But we didn't listen. We dared to reach out and ask these tall men to slap our hands when they rolled down the tunnel to the locker room.

Hearts pounded.

They were so tall.

We were such dorks.

There came one occasion where the four of us became separated from each other at game's end. Danny Sargent and I went to the meeting spot outside the Coliseum where the Dorans' father, Tom Doran, was to pick us up in a few minutes. Just then Seattle forward Spencer Haywood drove by in his Mercedes. We had seen with our own eyes an NBA player *driving a motor vehicle*. Right then, I knew what it must have been like to be a fan in the gym when Wilt scored his 100 points. Or when *Havlicek stole the ball*.

It was big all right. But the Dorans didn't believe us. "There is no way you saw Spencer Haywood," the twins said in unison. It's true, we protested. But Danny and I understood the Dorans' disbelief. Something that big, a true bond with a paid professional athlete, isn't supposed to happen. Not on that street. That's where twelve-year-olds are picked up by somebody's parents after a night playing hide-and-seek. How could we actually have been that close to a professional athlete? (It never dawned on us that we were standing by the only exit path from the players' parking lot.)

When the Sonics knocked down the title seven years later, we had grown up quite a bit. By then, we actually sat in our real seats the entire game. (Unless there was a huge block of wide-open seats in a nicer area. Come on, get real.) We no longer played hide-and-seek during the game. We had found what we were looking for. A different form of joy, expressed so eloquently when Gus and D.J. left the huddle early. When the building was their playpen.

Here's a relevant fact about basketball.

The 1978–79 Seattle Sonics were the first team to win an NBA championship without an eventual Hall of Fame player. The team's coach, Lenny Wilkens, was inducted as both a player and a coach.

Basketball: For Those Who Didn't Get Enough in the Previous Chapter

Some readers love basketball so much they yearn for more stories about the game, even stories written from the perspective of a guy who spent his youth playing hide-and-seek while Wilt Chamberlain was out on the floor dunking on Bob Rule. Those readers will love the fact that I mistakenly wrote a second basketball chapter. Or, if they hated the last chapter, the part about them loving this chapter won't be true. Readers who don't like basketball as much as those who love it can skip to the next chapter. Readers who neither love nor hate basketball can go on with what they were doing. Readers who just want words and don't care what the subject matter is can keep reading.

In basketball the Seattle Sonics have won one world championship. There are people from other countries who wonder how we call it a "world" championship when the only teams in competition for the title are from North America. When the Sonics won their title in 1979 there wasn't even one team from Canada. Nevertheless, it sounds way cooler to say "We are world champions" than it does to say "We are North American champions although there aren't any Canadian teams in the league yet."

When the Sonics were in the playoffs the season before their

Dennis Johnson   *Gus Williams*

North American Championship Although There Aren't Any Canadian Teams in the League Yet season I was attending junior college in Wenatchee, Washington. If I'm not mistaken, my college team won a league title the year before. They showed lots of class not calling it a North American title.

My friends Shawn Doran and the late Warren Thomas and I went to the Seattle Coliseum to support the team that would one day be North American champions. We bought three tickets from a scalper. One was directly behind the Portland Trail Blazers' bench. I mean you could reach out and snap Bill Walton's headband if you wanted to see how he felt about that. The other two seats were distant viewing. We did odd-man scissors, paper, rock to see who got to see Bill Walton's headband and who got to see the game from a thousand feet away. I won, or lost, depending on how you rate a seat that pretty much has you in the Blazers' huddle, but also with a view blocked by seven-foot-tall bench players.

Now that I know I duplicated my efforts with two basketball chapters, it's worth pointing out that (a) I did not use the first quarter to scout out better seats, because to be any closer would mean I was in the game, and as stated, I had no jumper, and (b) Shawn and I did not play hide-and-seek at halftime. I don't know if Shawn and Warren did.

All I know is, the next year the Sonics won the whole thing. By that time, I was attending UNLV. I watched the title game from a hotel lounge. This earned me great bragging rights. Not the part about the hotel lounge—anyone could go to those. The part about Seattle having won and me being from Seattle. When I did the bragging I did not bother to mention that I'm not really from Seattle. To do so I would have had to shout, "The Sonics are world champions or at least North American champions and I am from Kent, Washington!"

As exciting as it was to see Gus, D.J., Fred, Jack Sikma, and John Johnson help my city (can't believe Kent didn't get the franchise) win a North American championship, I knew the sport was also the root cause of one of my athletic low points.

The year was 1969. I was nine. At ten minutes to six on, I think, a Tuesday, Brian Foltz (much older, at age ten) called and said, "Can you get up to the school right away? We're two players short for the game!"

I now knew what it was like for a high-priced free agent to field the call from a professional ball club. A team was in need and I was the salvation. Not only that but a veteran player, a ten-year-old, had personally reached out to me. He must have told the head coach how he'd seen me on the playground and how I had just the right skills to push this team to the top. That, and the game started in less than ten minutes. That, and they were in such a need for top-flight players, they entrusted me to bring *anyone* with me.

I called Jeff Whidden. He lived two doors down. We lived, if sprinting, forty-five seconds from Star Lake Elementary. We met at the top of his driveway and ran to our school.

We were athletes.

We were warmly received. Of course we were. The team had just four players, and the league rules required that six be on site to avoid a forfeit. So what if we weren't the correct age (ten)? So what if our parents hadn't signed the parental permission slip? Years ahead of Magic and the Lakers it was: *show time!*

There was one problem.

Jeff had arrived wearing hiking boots, not basketball shoes. And one more problem: on the bottom of Jeff's hiking boots was dog poop. There was just one more problem: on the gym floor now there was smeared dog poop.

The game was held up for ten minutes while Jeff and I got paper towels and wiped the floor clean.

I don't remember who won. I do remember seeing the scorebook after the game and telling the coach proudly how "I didn't foul anyone!" The coach told me, "That means you didn't try very hard."

What an insult. I had personally prevented the team from suffering a humiliating forfeit, helped distribute the ball to the real scorers, and stayed out of foul trouble (can't have that with only six players, particularly when one of them has dog poop on his hiking boots), and I was being mocked for *not trying hard enough*?

This wasn't nearly as bad as having struck out off the tee in Really Lesser Little League (see "Baseball"), but the incident stayed with me for years. In fact, here it is, this year, in my coaster.

It seems appropriate that we print a picture at this juncture, or at least an illustration, as this whole sports thing is getting pretty dark.

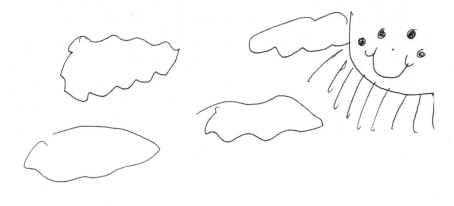

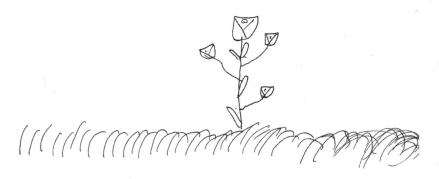

"Untitled" by Riley Mayne

Here's another relevant basketball fact.

Dr. James Naismith may have invented basketball, but he had a losing record as the head coach at the University of Kansas. He was 55–60 from 1898 to 1907.

Bocce

Until the day before I wrote this, I didn't know how to spell bocce. I thought it was bocci.

Bocci is a sport played in the back of Italian restaurants. The playing area is about the same size as in horseshoes, as is the feel of the game.

In bocci, the players toss balls from one end of the playing area, whatever that is called, to the other end. Players then walk to the end where their balls are and toss them to where they used to be.

In a perfect situation, one of the players in the game knows how to keep score so that the other person playing can figure out if what he or she did is good or bad. That way, the next time they play, they'll know how they can not lose the money they are now losing to the person who knows the rules on the night they don't.

The game is passed down from generation to generation.

I am fond of whole wheat pasta.

Here's a somewhat relevant fact about bocce.

Bocce ball dates back to ancient Egypt in 5200 B.C. Bocce ball was then picked up by the Greeks and Romans. The United States Bocce Federation was born in 1976, time enough to distance ourselves from the Romans.

Bowling

In bowling, Earl Anthony always won. He'd win every single time. We'd watch it on the black-and-white TV. Back in those days, families had one TV. Chris Schenkel, I think, announced everything.

Earl Anthony was from Tacoma, Washington, my birthplace. I felt connected, even though I didn't want to be a professional bowler. I figured if he could get on TV *just for bowling*, I could probably grow up to do something to get on TV.

My friends and I would go to Sea-Coma Lanes, named for the two major cities in the area, Seattle and Tacoma. I think the folks at Sea-Coma Lanes were trying to latch on to the Seattle name like I still do even though I'm really from Kent, Washington. We may have been over this topic already (P L A N A H), but it has more relevance this time. When you come right down to it, the bowling alley might have had a physical address of Milton, Washington.

Speaking of Milton, one cannot say or write Dave Krieg's name without noting that he is from *tiny Milton College, which no longer exists.* I'll leave space for you to try.

Dave Krieg, who is from tiny Milton College, which no longer exists, used to play tackle football for the Seahawks. He was a regular guy, who never tried to claim he was from Kent, Washington. Just Wisconsin, where he liked to hunt and fish. I don't know about bowling.

In bowling, you rented dirty shoes that were usually dyed red. The guy behind the counter sometimes sprayed the shoes with disinfectant, but you didn't care, you were ten years old. The only germs that mattered were girl germs. Next you walked around and tried to find a light ball suitable for throwing down the lane as hard as possible, but not so hard as to necessitate a visit to Dr. James Andrews, of Birmingham, Alabama, who, like Dave Krieg, who is from tiny Milton College, which no longer exists, cannot be mentioned without noting that he is *of* Birmingham, Alabama, which does still exist.

I'll now leave space for you to try to write Dr. James Andrews of Birmingham, Alabama, without noting the part about "of Birmingham, Alabama." It can't be done. At least not on *SportsCenter*.

Once the correctly weighted bowling ball had been found, suitable for throwing as hard as possible, but without necessitating a visit to Dr. James Andrews of Birmingham, Alabama, it was time to go to the snack machine and buy something awful for you. This could be accomplished by pressing any of the letter-number combo buttons because everything inside the vending machine had a half-life of three thousand years, whatever half-life means.

You would then return to your lane, in your nondisinfected shoes, punch your buddy on the arm if he didn't laugh at your jokes, settle into your chair, and start making up bowler names for the scorecard.

Just then, you would get up because you had forgotten to purchase pop (pop or soda, the question separates our people). The pop machines in those days dispensed a tiny red Coca-Cola cup and a mixture of syrup and carbonated water flowed into the cup and it could all be had for *ten cents*. And damn it, it was good. So you would drink one cup, then another, right there at the pop machine.

You'd buy a third and bring it back with you to the little table at the head of the bowling-ball-return machine and begin arguing with your friends over who got to be which professional bowler on the scorecard.

I've pretty much forgotten all the other professional bowlers' names from that era except for Earl Anthony, who, as you are aware, was born in Tacoma. Maybe he was born elsewhere but lived in Tacoma. I really don't care at this point and neither should you. Just trust me when I say it was a big deal to be Earl Anthony. We would settle the argument with scissors, paper, rock. (Which, as mentioned, but not as often as Earl Anthony's birthplace, was the way I learned to say the name of the game. It was a public-school education for me.)

So, somebody would be Earl Anthony and the others would be somebody else, sometimes their actual name, which was stupid, I know, but we had to chart the scores because we would remember the results for at least ten minutes after we were done.

We would throw the ball (often one of those "star" balls) as hard as possible, sometimes halfway down the lane in the air, resulting in a thudding sound that would draw the attention of the guy who hadn't disinfected our shoes very well, so who was he to judge us when he wasn't exactly Mr. Rule Follower to begin with?

We would finish up when we ran out of money or when it was time for someone's mom to come and pick us up, unless we walked home, but that was a long walk in that we were way out there in Milton, Washington, or whatever that place was called. On those occasions when we did walk home we would walk north, away from Tacoma and Milton and toward Seattle. We weren't hung up yet on calling Seattle home. Matter of fact, I'm over it. Right now. The kids up there in Seattle may have looked down on us for being from Kent. But I am sure they went bowling too.

And they did so nowhere near Earl Anthony.

Here's a relevant fact about bowling.

In December 2006, Chaz Dennis became the youngest bowler ever to roll a 300 game (as approved by the United States Bowling Congress, which is just like the U.S. House of Representatives, I think). His age of ten years, two months, twenty-seven days was twenty days younger than the previous record holder's. Dennis rolled his 300 game during his Preps-Juniors League at Hillcrest Lanes in Columbus, Ohio.

Boxing

The date was.

I don't remember the date. I know it was October of 1980 and I know I was about to break my leg in tackle football. Again.

I didn't know it then. Not on that date that I don't know. If I had known it, when it came time to break my leg, I would have taken a knee. I mean, we were down to Oregon something like 32–9, with just seconds remaining in the game. I may not be a big stats guy, but I'm certain that in 1980 they had no plays worth 24 points. Things may have changed.

I'm going to guess the date was October 5, 1980. As promised, this book is being handled with no research whatsoever. It would be a long walk up to my office to check the date. The date is right there on the usher's shirt under the glass case. If I were to get up to check the date I'd have to move from the couch and from under the bag of ice which is again atop my right and ruined ankle, from the break I suffered for not taking a knee. I guess I could minimize this Word thing and search around on the Internet, but what if I hit the wrong button and lose everything I've done so far? Plus, the Internet is going out of style. Total fad.

Damn it, I should have taken a knee at Oregon.

A couple weeks earlier, on October 5 (I guess), I was as healthy as I could be, the best shape of my life.

It's no wonder The Man chose me for such an important assignment.

The Man was the guy who seemed to be in charge of the entire

Muhammad Ali entourage. Big entourage. This guy must have been important.

I was one of thirty or so tackle football players who'd been invited to usher the Ali-Holmes heavyweight title fight. UNLV was big on NCAA compliance so we weren't allowed to be paid for the assignment. But what twenty-year-old college junior would require to be paid to *watch Muhammad Ali in one of his final fights?*

Michael Morton and Ray Crouse, that's who. They weren't on the payroll, for that would have been an NCAA rules violation. But they certainly knew how to create a payday. They ran back and forth from the concession stands all night long for the high-priced-ticket holders. Those folks had already forked over something in the thousands for ringside seats, so what was the change from a hundred-dollar bill to them if they received their four beers?

I went a different path. I wanted to see the fight. Once I carried out The Man's orders, I took a knee five feet from Jack Nicholson and watched the main event. I'd already pocketed a few hundred in tips for merely walking people to their seats and dusting them off with a towel. The seats that is, not the people. Not that the seats were all that dusty. I mean, this fight was in the Caesars Palace back parking lot, not in somebody's attic. But the very act of pretending to dust off the seat created that awkward tipping scenario delay between the time of semiservice and serviceperson's exit. The customers would dust me off with a twenty. (I could have been a valet or doorman. See "Australian Rules Football.")

Long before I took a knee next to Jack and said something stupid like "I loved you in *Cuckoo's Nest,*" I'd already been in a fight of my own.

During the undercard fight before Ali and Holmes, one of the lead ushers instructed a handful of us to head toward the Ali trailer. The former champ and his people would be coming down to the ring soon, and able-bodied tackle football players were needed for extra manpower. Somehow the guy pointed to me and ordered me out of the ringside-seat area. This new assignment threatened to cause me financial hardship. I was making tens and twenties right and left, dusting off seats like a great sandstorm had just blown through town. Being compelled to leave was a huge letdown until it was revealed to me that I had a once-in-a-lifetime opportunity. Muhammad Ali needed me.

I saw Ali in his trailer when the door was opened a bit. He appeared to be meditating. I met up with The Man, the guy in charge of the compound and Ali's people. There was security everywhere.

And then there was me.

The Man sized me up and somehow came away impressed. "I'm going to assign you to a very important person," he told me. He didn't tell me who but I was pretty certain it wasn't Ali. This was a letdown because to be on escort detail for anyone but Ali was definitely a second-rate position.

Then I saw her.

Nabila Khashoggi, the daughter of billionaire Adnan Khashoggi, who years later would be made known to Americans in the Iran-Contra scandal.

All I knew was she was the most beautiful thing I had ever seen. She appeared to be about my age, but far more refined. A billion or two will do that for you. I had a few hundred in my pocket, everything I owned.

I was told her name and that she was very, very important. "Don't lose track of her," The Man said.

The signal came that the Ali entourage was about to move toward the ring.

Minutes later, *I lost track of her.*

There must have been a hundred people or more in the entourage, and many more jumped on board for the ride. We didn't so much walk toward the ring as be carried along a wave of pressure, a wave of raw energy. The music blared, the crowd was on its feet. Muhammad Ali was on his way to the ring.

So was I.

So was Nabila.

Wherever the hell she was.

The surge of the crowd pulled Nabila away and in a flash she was ten feet in front of me being carried toward the ring by the crush of this procession.

I panicked. *Do not lose track of her.*

I still didn't know exactly who she was. I just knew she was connected to Ali. She looked like a princess.

She looked so pretty, so fragile, so vulnerable.

She looked to be about fifteen feet in front of me now.

I rammed my way through the crowd, through men larger than me, through the armed security personnel. I found my way to Nabila's side about fifty yards from the ring. I put my hands on her shoulders, apologized for getting separated from her. I nearly picked her up and carried her at one point. I never lost track of her again.

We got to her seats, where she was joined by a couple of men she knew.

But there were people in the seats.

I didn't judge them for it. I'd made a living as a child spotting better seats than those I'd paid for at Seattle Sonics games. But this was Ali-Holmes. This was Nabila Khashoggi. I waved to a police officer for backup but did the job alone. The intruders left, using the "We must have read our tickets wrong" defense.

Nabila thanked me for my dedicated service. I felt like a hero.

I watched the fight with one eye on Nabila.

I watched Larry Holmes show equal concern for Ali. Holmes could have hurt the former champ but he held his punches. Ali was not the same fighter I'd grown up watching. Ali did not come out for the eleventh round.

The entourage disbanded after the fight. Its members scattered away from the ring in small groups or alone.

Nabila still had me. We talked a little. About what I have no idea. She was out of my league. A princess. I was a backup quarterback about to break my leg.

The Man thanked me for returning Nabila safely to the compound. I held up some pedestrians so she could get into her limo and drive away. She smiled.

The Man handed me a one-hundred-dollar bill, a fortune to a college junior.

The next day The Man called to invite me out on the town with Nabila and another friend. We ended up going to see Wayne Newton. Nabila looked bored. We talked some more. About what I have no idea. I had her autograph my losing fifty-dollar betting slip for the wager I'd placed on Ali.

It's faded a bit after all these years. But it's still there, in the glass case with the usher's shirt. It looks a lot like the signature of a princess.

I've never lost track of it.

Here's a relevant fact about boxing.

Muhammad Ali (formerly Cassius Clay) wasn't the only heavyweight champ to change his name. Rocky Marciano was born Rocco Marchegiano, Jersey Joe Walcott was Arnold Cream, and Jack Sharkey was Joseph Zukauskas. I had no idea this book would take such a serious tone.

Car Racing

Car racing is when you're on the freeway, already doing seventy-five in a fifty-five and some guy who thinks he's Dale Earnhardt gets all over you, and pretty much attaches himself to your bumper. He starts flashing his high beams. Problem is, you can't see that he's flashing his high beams because he's on top of you.

Now he's honking his horn. There's a truck carrying poultry to your right and a hippie van in the distance, doing fifty-seven in the fast lane. Once you clear the truck carrying poultry, and right before you're on top of the hippie van doing fifty-seven, you swing to the middle lane and give Earnhardt what he wanted.

Go ahead and have it, Dale. I'm now going to drop down to fifty-seven because maybe I care about safety and the environment. The fast lane is yours.

For those who tried to box in the real Earnhardt, on the real track, they had to know he wasn't worried about the presence of a state trooper or even NASCAR. There weren't (and aren't) a lot of rules.

In fact, the strangest of the unwritten rules in car racing is the one drivers all claim to abide by with regard to spinning or not spinning the lead car off of turn four on the final lap of a race. They claim to play things fair and square, and it's true that as recently as the spring of 2007 I saw it play out in a gentlemen's way when both Jeff Burton and Jeff Gordon had chances to win a race by spinning the lead car but elected to play things safe and settled for second place.

Then again, I've seen dozens of races when in pursuit of victory a driver didn't heed this unwritten rule. The double standard during the postrace arguments is that the same move that is labeled "daring" (when the pass is made without spinning the leader) is called "reckless" (when the pass sends the leader sideways and worse). The guy who thinks he's about to win, but takes a nudge that has him finishing not in first but upside down, and maybe on fire, is the guy who is sounding off later about how the guy who gave the nudge, won the race, didn't end up on fire, is somehow playing outside the *rules*.

It would have sucked to have Dale Earnhardt behind your cart at the grocery store. You're moving down aisle five, looking for the *exact* kind of paprika your wife listed for use in the chicken paprikash (it must be *Hungarian paprika* and no other). It turns out Earnhardt's wife is making the same dish this night. It's bad enough he chose to bump draft, but in this case it means your ankles take the blow. You're bruised and might be bleeding, your cart is sideways into the canned soup. Earnhardt has passed you by. He gets the last can of Hungarian paprika. He gets the victory. He has earned his dinner.

And that's pretty much car racing in a nutshell. They drive as though the others are trying to take away their dinner. If every American worker had it in his or her head each day that dinner was on the line, we'd have a more productive workforce. I think Milton Friedman said that.

Earnhardt went out there and took away food. He left a whole bunch of drivers hungry.

And then he died.

How did that happen? Dale Earnhardt died driving a car? That doesn't hardly make sense. He was the one who was supposed to be sending others into the wall. We sort of thought Dale Earnhardt would drive as long as he pleased, take away some more dinners, go fishing. That was supposed to be it.

But as tough as he seemed on the exterior, and this is cliché—and the computer lets you know when you're using a cliché because it automatically puts the little squiggly thing over the word when you write it down; in fact, I think my computer was about to write the word "cliché" *and* put the squiggly thing over the word just as I was starting to type—*he had a softer side.*

But he did.

As little as I knew the man, one night on his boat proved it.

The year before (1998), he'd won the Daytona 500 for the first and last time. We had a little tradition going at ESPN of inviting the defending champ to cohost the *SportsCenter* segments the following year.

Earnhardt had already made a big impression on our studio the night he won the 500. He walked into our trackside studio, a glass of champagne in his hand, and looked at me. "Are you still dating Jeff Gordon?"

I had nothing. Just bright red.

I hadn't actually been dating Jeff Gordon but had been sticking him on the TV in assorted ways. He was the driver of the future then; Earnhardt was the driver of the past, competitive as he still was. It made sense to us, anyway. Besides his killer line, what struck me as funny was that Earnhardt was actually keeping track. And his point was well taken. We'd forgotten a bit about the guy who was still taking away dinners. We'd latched on to the spectacular new star and forgotten about the proven old vet. On that night, Earnhardt was king once more. He'd taken down the Daytona 500 in his twentieth attempt.

I asked him to sign a little trading card for a future charity event. I'd been paid by a trading-card company to write short stories (on Earnhardt, I used the grocery store analogy) about each of the drivers. Earnhardt, the first to really exploit his brand among drivers, looked over the card and accused me of copyright infringement. After the Gordon comment, I didn't know if he was serious or not, so I tried to withdraw the request. But Earnhardt grabbed the card and signed it. Then he asked that I sign something for him, why I don't know.

We were live on the satellite but not yet on the air. I'd put in a call to a Secret Service agent I knew in the White House to see if we could back-channel a phone call to the president (Clinton) and have him come on the air and congratulate Dale for the 500 victory. As I apprised him of what was going on Dale blurted out, "Hell no. He's a womanizer." I think he was just screwing with the president, as he was with me, but we didn't have to suffer a confrontation, since the president did not make the call.

A year later Dale served as cohost at Daytona. During a break he asked if I wanted to come over and have dinner with him on his boat, *Sunday Money.* Recalling his manner from the previous year, I was certain he was completely messing with me. I'd say yes, he'd say he was just kidding. Who are you to think I would invite you to my boat? But it would have been rude to take it that way so I said sure, how do I get there? In front of twenty to thirty people in the studio and a satellite connection, he offered up his cell phone number.

With Dale and his wife, Teresa, we dined on some kind of white fish, shared a bottle of wine (Earnhardt drank wine?), and looked through picture books of their family. At about 9 p.m., Dale said he had to run off to some kind of publicity event. He told me to stay and look at some more pictures with Teresa. But as he started through the door, he turned back and said, "But don't stay *too long.*"

Before that remark, he was downright *sweet.* I know this will blow it for some of his fans, but it's the truth. I'd been fighting a cold all week and was sneezing and sniffling through the evening. Dale brought me one cold treatment after another. He talked about his favorite ways to fight a cold. He recommended more rest. *He nursed me.*

I expected him to give me a hard time for being such a wimp about the cold. I figured he'd tell me to be a man about it and shake it off. Instead, he gave it considered thought as to the best cold remedy. He said, "Let me know if this works, or we'll try something else tomorrow."

Dale Earnhardt: *intimidator.*

I looked through the pictures with Teresa. Nice-looking family, but I didn't want to linger. I didn't want to cross the man who had *provided me dinner.*

There's a long list of guys who ended up hungry racing Dale Earnhardt. Here's hoping some of them were fed, at least once, some of Dale's compassion.

Here's a relevant fact about car racing.

Dale Earnhardt won a record thirty-four lifetime races at Daytona International Speedway but just one Daytona 500. He won six IROC events, one of which was in a pink car.

Carnival Games

If hot-dog-eating contests are on TV sports channels, why are carnival-game athletes getting the shaft?

It takes just as much skill to land a dime on a greasy plate as it does to land a four-foot putt, yet no one is questioning whether Tiger is an athlete.

As for the balls-thrown section of the carnival arcade, there's no question many *ex-athletes* have been involved.

Usually they are over thirty-five, balding, and have three or four kids in tow and a wife who has seen it all before. She was there when the guy played high school tackle football. She was there when he recounted the glory of high school tackle football. All 788 times.

And now here he is at the stand. The barker lured him in with "Don't you want to win the little kiddies a big prize?"

He puts down a twenty. That buys him eight throws. He must hit all eight to win the grand prize, the big-assed stuffed animal that will have to be mounted on the hood of the car, like a deer, if it is to make it home.

To miss even once means the kids go home with, at best, one of the medium-size stuffed animals.

With no warmup tosses whatsoever, he launches the first throw. It crashes into the plate, sending porcelain in all directions. The game master pulls some of it from his throat and nods to the ex-athlete.

The second, third, and fourth throws are all good. The children are all smiles. The plates break apart, one after the other.

The ex-athlete is adored by his children. They look up and see

Nolan Ryan. His wife scouts with her eyes for the Hall of Home Improvement—it's two down from the blue ribbon cattle.

The fifth throw glances off the plate. It doesn't move.

There will be no jumbo prize.

Our thrower sinks into depression. The look on the faces of his children cuts him deep. He throws the sixth and seventh balls as hard as possible, knocking down just one more plate.

The medium-size stuffed animal is awarded. The kids argue over whose room it will go into.

The wife stares. The father will not be able to lift his right arm for three days.

Hell, yes. He's an athlete.

The greatest depiction ever of carnival game depression and elation came in the film In America.

Here is a relevant fact about carnival games.

On the Web site www.occupationalinfo.com, which was just underlined, as though you can be linked to it right now, you can receive information about a career in carnival games.

Cheadle Incident

The question I'm asked most often, besides "Can I have an ESPN hat?" is "Who was the coolest person you've ever interviewed?"

That's easy. Stevie Wonder. The other guys I've encountered just play sports.

Stevie and I actually collaborated on some music way back in 1986. It's still unreleased.

I was on maybe my third day of TV reporting in Seattle when I talked the producers into sending me to Stevie's rehearsal for his "In Square Circle" tour. Seattle was the first stop. The man in charge, Stevie's brother, Milton Hardaway, told the media there'd be no interview session. We were allowed to tape five minutes of the sound check and get out. The five minutes became ten, then fifteen. I was just happy to be there. Being in Stevie's presence was enough. But one of the more enterprising reporters decided to walk up onto the stage and start firing questions at Stevie. At that point, given Stevie's willingness to stop down and answer questions, the rules about our conduct were entirely thrown out, and the rest of us less ambitious reporters and cameramen climbed onto the stage as well. My photographer and I were in the back of the old Seattle Coliseum when the rules of engagement changed, so we ended up with a bad angle for the ad hoc press conference. As Stevie was deep into an answer, I squeezed my handheld microphone toward him so as to pick up some sound. In doing so, partly because of my bad angle and partly because my nervous hand was shaking, I laid my mic on Stevie's keyboard. Suddenly, a low note was struck. Stevie just kept talking. I realized what I had done but even before I could lift my mic off the keys, Stevie reached over and turned down the volume.

To this day I can say, "I jammed with Stevie Wonder."

I reminded Stevie of this when I got to interview him before Super Bowl XL in Detroit. He replied, "Good. Let's make the album."

That was my second encounter (or third, if you count the jam session) with Stevie.

The other came in the summer of 2005, Philadelphia, Pennsylvania. Stevie was the headliner there for the American contribution to Live 8, the music-driven campaign led by Bono to get the industrialized nations to forgive debt and otherwise give Africa some love.

A couple weeks later, I was to play again in the Legends-Celebrities softball game for ESPN at the All-Star Weekend in Detroit. Stevie grew up in Saginaw, Michigan, so I sold my producer, Tim Scanlan, on the following: I would go to Philadelphia on one day's notice, acquire a press pass to Live 8, and try to get Stevie Wonder to say, "Sorry I can't be at the All-Star game. I have a high ankle sprain." In that ESPN clears about two billion dollars a year, I figured what's the cost of a flight, hotel, rental car, and a camera crew to get Stevie Wonder's inclusion in our made-for-television softball game? Most senior producers would worry about the budget, and I had to admit to Scan that the chances of getting Stevie were slim. He said, "Go for it. I think you'll pull it off."

In Philadelphia the night before the concert I went to the office of the show's organizers. They gave me press credentials for me and my crew. These credentials allowed us to be in a press tent, about five hundred yards away from the show and with little or no shot at getting Stevie Wonder to drop his line.

A couple hours before the show was to begin, I took a walk toward the concert stage. A bunch of Teamsters were helping set up the stage and one of them asked me what I was up to. I explained to him my quest and within minutes I was handed a backstage pass. This trumped my flimsy paper-thin press pass that allowed me into a tent five hundred yards away from the show. My cameraman and audio tech didn't get the same upgrades, but one of the players in Maroon 5 said the right things to a security guard and suddenly three guys who were supposed to be in a tent five hundred yards from the concert were now hanging out in the VIP section behind the stage, in position to land Stevie Wonder. Unfortunately, another one of the security guards thought he was CIA and tried to run us. We brokered a deal with him that we'd stay in one place, not bother the stars, and wait for Stevie Wonder's arrival.

When Stevie arrived and entered his trailer, his right-hand man periodically came outside and waved this or that star to come in and meet with Stevie. Will Smith got the invite. Then later it was Adam Levine of Maroon 5, who would also get to sing with Stevie on stage. Natalie Portman was waved into Stevie's trailer, and several others who mattered.

I stood staring at Stevie's trailer, just happy to take in his aura. Then the right-hand man looked right at me. Big smile. He pointed in my direction and smiled even bigger. Then he waved, as if to invite me into Stevie's trailer.

I froze. I thought to myself, "There is no way Stevie Wonder knows who I am." Then I had a second thought. Maybe the right-hand man was some kind of big sports fan and was just being extra cool about it. I could imagine the introduction. "Stevie, this is Kenny Mayne. I watch him every morning on *SportsCenter*. He's one of your biggest fans."

Just as that thought and twenty more were flying around in my head, and just as I took the slightest step forward to the trailer and this smiling, happily waving man, *Don Cheadle walked by me and into Stevie's trailer.*

The actor had been standing over my shoulder the entire time. He had seen the smiling, happily waving right-hand man too. I wonder why it took Don Cheadle so long to know the smiling and waving was for him.

Given that the smiling and waving were connected to an audience with Stevie Wonder, maybe Don Cheadle wondered if he was worthy.

Four hours later the right-hand man heard my pitch. He was no longer smiling and waving. He was tired. There's a lot of energy expended being Stevie Wonder's right-hand man. He told me I could have one minute to explain to Stevie the bit and then "it'll be up to Stevie if he wants to do it."

I told Stevie Wonder that I'm the guy who knows all the lyrics to *Journey Through the Secret Life of Plants*. I explained the Detroit All-Star Game–Saginaw background connection.

He killed his line in one take.

Childbirth

As my wife, Laura, was busy pushing out our first girl I looked at her with awe. She alone was doing all the work. She alone was responsible for assisting our baby Riley Hope gain her first breaths outside the womb. I felt so useless. All I'd done is have sex with Laura on a Monopoly board (in a trade for giving her Park Place—I don't regret the transaction at all, even though she already owned Boardwalk). I stood there in my hospital garb, and said things such as "Breathe, breathe, breathe." We'd gone to birthing class together a half dozen times.

A total waste of time.

We did not apply one single thing learned (or forgotten) from that class. Such classes are useful only to those who end up having a baby in the backseat of a car or in the mountains, for all the many pregnant women who set out hiking at thirty-nine weeks of gestation.

I remember on the way to the hospital saying the single dumbest thing I hope I will ever utter: "Laura, there's going to be a minor amount of pain, but I'll be right there for you."

You think?

The contractions were starting to come more often and with greater intensity. We still had a few miles on our drive to the hospital. I just thought I should say something calming. Instead, I said *that*. Laura didn't say anything in response. She simply looked at me and thought to herself: "How did I not get Marvin Gardens and all the utilities?"

The labor wasn't really that bad.

For me.

Things slowed down a bit once we arrived at the hospital. Nurses came in and out of the room and took Laura's blood pressure and said appropriate things. Dr. Rotis was on the day shift. He looked a lot like Jeff Goldblum. (Loved him in *Jurassic Park*.) The dinosaur involved this time was the doctor coming on at the end of Goldblum's shift. We'd had some issues with that guy. He had no bedside manner at all and we were looking for Marcus Welby during the pregnancy checkups in that we'd lost our twin sons Creighton and Connor three years previous, and had suffered two miscarriages since then.

One day that doctor looked over an ultrasound scan of Riley. We were maybe four or five months into the project. After a long and unnerving pause he asked us: "Do you know what the chances are that you'll have a Down baby?" We didn't know what he meant. Given our experience, we definitely had a fear of anything else going wrong with this pregnancy (and this is meant as no disrespect to Down children). After what seemed like a full minute of silence, he broke the news that there was very little chance of the baby suffering Down syndrome. I saw how scared Laura was during the silence (and knew how scared I was). I saw how the announcement that everything was okay didn't really cheer her up, as she had been taken to the cliff once again. With this doctor's inept delivery of this "good news" he had ruined the occasion of a healthy report on the baby at the halfway point of pregnancy.

I said to him: "So as opposed to opening with something to scare the hell out of us, you could have instead simply told us the pictures and heartbeat are in perfect order, right? You could have led with optimism."

He mumbled yes.

We left that room hoping to never see him again. There were five doctors in the practice, so we had an 80 percent chance of not having to deal with him on delivery day.

But there he was coming on shift. Fear came over Laura, anger came over me. Dr. Goldblum sensed our discomfort, put off a night with his family, and stayed five hours past his shift time to deliver Riley Hope Mayne.

The doctors and nurses looked her over and gave her an Apgar assessment, which is the numerical score on the mini physical given newborns. They didn't bother telling us the number. The pediatrician in the room just said, "She is *perfect.*"

About thirty minutes before that pronouncement, when I was saying important things such as "Breathe, breathe, breathe," I looked at Laura in a way I'd never looked at her (the delivery of the twins was too great a blur to recall all of it). Not that I'd treated Laura poorly before. But right there, with my child's welfare entirely in Laura's hands, I felt more love and respect for her than words can impart. And that's saying a lot, since this is a book.

I remember thinking, "I will never get mad at this girl again. There is nothing she can do after doing *this* that will ever be disagreeable to me."

I broke that promise. People say and think some crazy things in that delivery room.

Sixteen months later, Laura pulled it off again. This one was a real easy labor. No. Really, she'll tell you herself. One minute we were watching *Law & Order,* the next minute they're telling her to push the baby out. It was over in ten minutes. We missed a great episode but ended up with Anna Yvonne Mayne.

At night, when all three are asleep and I'm still up reading or writing, I sometimes stare at them. It's my most content time of any day. It is at that time when I almost live up to that delivery room promise. It's at that time when I know each of them can do nothing that I would find disagreeable.

Here is a relevant fact about childbirth.

The average length of labor is between twelve and fifteen hours for a first pregnancy and about eight hours in subsequent pregnancies. With regard to ten-minute labors, if anyone has a copy of the *Law & Order* that aired on January 10, 2001, please contact me.

Coaching

My daughters were paid $150 for the illustrations you see throughout this book. Keep in mind, I also pay for their food and clothing. Matter of fact, Riley just earned $2 to help me stack wood. Annie banked $9 because she stayed on board for the entire project. Riley went inside early claiming an illness. Twenty minutes later, she was able to muster the energy to come back outside when I gave the girls "Disneyland" rides in their little stick handle blue plastic car.

The noise the car's plastic wheels make when they go over the cobblestones just off our driveway replicates the chain noise of a roller coaster on the incline. The stick handle blue plastic car is something Laura and I intend to keep forever. It was the first vehicle we purchased for Riley.

Another thing we will keep forever is the kindergarten journal each child wrote during her time in Ms. Herlihy's class. We love Ms. Herlihy, as do the girls. She teaches all the basics but also adds in Spanish, sign language, a kindergarten "Idol" year-end show, and a class party for this or that reason about every four days.

Ms. Herlihy has her students keep a journal even though most of them can barely spell their own name.

This is good practice, much in the same way my junior-high shop teacher had me do projects even though I'm an idiot. Truth be told, the shop teacher at Totem Junior High saw the exact same hand trowel in three successive quarters. First, Dennis Doran made one expertly and received an A for his grade. His brother Shawn, whose aptitude for shop rivaled mine, turned in the same trowel the next quarter and received a B. By the time the hand trowel was passed down to me, either the teacher was onto this scam or he'd stiffened his grading judgment. If he was onto us, I should have received an F for cheating, but instead I pulled a C. This was far better than the D I would have gotten for turning in a glob of unformed metal because there is not a chance in the world I could have made anything approximating the hand trowel Dennis Doran crafted, if indeed he did.

There is only one other occasion in my academic career in which I cheated, and for that I feel bad to this day.

We'll get to my daughters soon. They're not going anywhere. They are asleep.

Before enrolling at UNLV in 1979, I received an associate arts degree from Wenatchee Valley Community College in Wenatchee, Washington. I was compelled to attain my A.A. degree from Wenatchee before transferring to another Division I-A football school, as previous to Wenatchee I had walked on (and off) at the University of Washington in 1977. I didn't really think I was going to beat out future Hall of Famer Warren Moon, but at the same time I thought I was better than the freshman quarterback who was on scholarship. While he got to take reps with the fourth-team offense, actual tackle football players, I worked alone on the sidelines, sometimes without even a ball, going through my footwork. The other walk-on dorks and I worked against air to improve our technique. At least that's what the quarterbacks coach said we were doing. Personally, I thought the whole exercise was a cousin of make-believe slow-motion football every child plays while listening to college football on the radio at age nine (for me it was Bob Robertson calling Washington State games) via AM on the family console stereo.

You didn't?

So I *walked off* at Washington and enrolled at Wenatchee Valley, where after one fairly successful season I left school to field offers from four-year schools who would have a six-two, 170-pound quarterback.

I went bowling one night, long before my daughters wrote their kindergarten journals for Ms. Herlihy's class, and a fellow bowler two lanes over approached me and asked if I would like to be a garbageman. Nothing against garbagemen—they are far more necessary than book writers—but I thought I was on my way to big-time college tackle football.

Then the guy, Steve Caputo, told me the job paid sixteen dollars per hour. It was too much to pass up.

I took the job to save up some money until I'd transfer to the four-year school in the spring. I handled some Seattle garbage routes on those days when the regular garbageman for a particular route failed to show up for work. I did this for a couple months as the offers began to pour in.

One offer.

Montana was interested and so was I. It was Division I-AA but at least it wasn't community college.

But the deal was queered when the quarterbacks coach there informed me that my five days of running fake plays on Warren Moon's sideline designated me as a "four-year school" transfer student. This, even though I never even attended classes at Washington. I had to earn a community college degree before I could transfer to another Division I-A or I-AA school.

Oh.

For having suffered through the Pac-10's caste system, I now had to earn a community college degree in three quarters in order to move on to a tackle football school as I'd always hoped. I made some money taking away people's trash, the most significant trash being that thrown out by Lori Beiberstein, a cute girl from my high school. Early one morning in West Seattle I walked down an alley past her bathroom window with my large silver garbage can.

She poked her head out the window and called out my name. I don't know why I was embarrassed—we'd been nothing more than friends. It could have been one of those moments when, at the sight of a pretty girl, and in the middle of another grueling morning lifting people's garbage away to a diesel-powered truck, while wondering why I didn't stay at Washington and play on the freshman team and maybe beat out the guy who would eventually be moved to receiver, and be on the travel team for the Rose Bowl—and to add yet another clause to a ridiculously long sentence—I could have become emboldened to break free from this life and go back to community college and earn that A.A. degree, but instead I just said, "I'm your garbageman."

I haven't seen Lori Beiberstein since.

I did go back to Wenatchee the next quarter, and I played another season there the following fall. And I did earn my A.A. degree. I did this by challenging Spanish (*muy fácil*) and by taking night classes such as Math for Everyday Living.

Math for Everyday Living wasn't recognized by UNLV as worthy of science credits. To this day, I do not see why not.

So, coming into my final senior semester at UNLV, I was informed I still needed one science credit to get my B.A. in broadcasting.

I took geology. That is to say, I signed up for geology. I even went to class on the first day. But other than the first day, I didn't step foot into the geology class until the *last day*. I did go on the field trip to the mountains outside of Las Vegas. There was going to be one cute girl on the bus. She didn't hold a candle to Lori Beiberstein.

On the last day, I showed up to take the one test. Pass or Fail. It would give me the one science credit I lacked to graduate on time.

I failed.

I took the advice of a friend in class who said the supposedly cute girl on the field-trip bus was also the smartest person ever. All I had to do was glance at her multiple-choice answers and the credits would be mine.

Except for the eighth-grade shop class hand trowel conspiracy, I had never cheated on a test. I had studied hard for a few days. I thought I knew the material well enough to pull a C, a passing grade. I walked into the class fairly confident. Then my friend advised me how I could have full confidence by cheating off the semicute girl.

I had some guilt during the pretest time about taking another's answers.

Then I took her answers.

She would mark B when I thought the answer was C. She'd put an X on A when I thought it was D. She had no idea what she was doing. That much I am still sure of. She had no idea what the answers were on *my test*. This is because we were taking different tests. The professor had been around the block. He knew about the kind of student who challenges Spanish in junior college to expedite an A.A. degree. The kind of student who shows up to the field trip solely because there might be another Lori Beiberstein in the universe.

The bastard had handed out alternating multiple-choice tests.

I had flunked.

I had not graduated.

This put me in something of a bind when my grandmother was handing out thousand-dollar checks to anyone who had graduated that December. Certainly wasn't me. But I didn't want to spoil it for her. She looked so proud. I took the check. But I knew I had lied. I wished I could be picking up Lori Beiberstein's garbage. *I was Lori Beiberstein's garbage.*

I went back to UNLV. I took a computer science class. I got my science credits. I got my degree. I have not cheated on a test since.

I have not taken any tests since.

I did sort of cheat once more. It was something of a writing test. My television station in Seattle was KSTW, which itself had cheated in saying it was a Seattle station when its headquarters office was in Tacoma (why is every American company a "Delaware Corporation"?). KSTW was putting out a cookbook for charity. All the employees were asked to turn in their favorite recipes. I thought I would stick it to the Man by making up an entire recipe out of whole cloth (and some words).

The book was not copyrighted. Plus, I wrote it and wasn't compensated. So here it is, in full.

Catfish Orange
by Kenny Mayne

4 catfish
4 oranges
1 white onion
1 green pepper, large
Tabasco sauce

Clean fish. Fresh-squeeze oranges. (Frozen juice may be substituted.) Put juice in small saucepan, set aside. Peel and chop onion. Chop pepper. Measure one cup Tabasco. Set oven on bake at 450 degrees. Place fish, onion, and pepper into baking dish and smother with Tabasco. Bake 30 minutes. Ten minutes prior to removing fish, place orange juice on medium heat, stir constantly. When orange juice thickens and reaches boiling point, empty into bowl and place into freezer. Let stand five minutes. Take out and pour over fish. Serves four.

I was later told by my friend photographer Jan Kuwahara that his wife attended a YMCA cooking class. The instructor handed out the cookbook with the warning, "Under no circumstances should anyone even attempt to make Catfish Orange."

I ask, who is to say Wendy Mann's Norwegian Spritz wasn't a complete fabrication?

And while we're at it, who is to say my daughters didn't make up a lot of stuff in their kindergarten journals? And what was Ms. Herlihy doing forcing my daughters to write back when they could barely read?

From Annie's journal, dated March 29, 2007: "I wint to school thin I wint to ESPN thin we piket up pizza."

How did Annie know how to spell "school" but not "went"?

Ms. Herlihy added a note: "Sounds like a great day!" Who is Ms. Herlihy to endorse a day in which my six-year-old was forced to go to work with me on a day that was not sanctioned officially as "Bring Your Daughter to Work Day" and then be handed cheese on top of crust for dinner?

From Riley's journal, dated April 12, 2005: "I had a fun day. I mad a bech [book]. My mom gav me a manakara [manicure] and we rad your book. I men we rad your book. Riley."

Ms. Herlihy added a note: "I got a manicure yesterday too!" And she told Riley, "Great job" with respect to Riley's note about rading her book.

How did Riley get a "great job" for repeating the same sentence with the same spelling error on the word "rad" (read)?

What has happened to our educational system?

Okay. I cheated. I was wrong. The girl wasn't even that cute.

From Annie's journal, dated March 27, 2007: "I wint to school thin I road the bus home thin I road my bike and I fell don on the same neey. My mom took care of me agaen."

This would be considered cute until the entry for the next day was made: "I wint to school my sister was sik. Thin me and my sister playd owt sid. We hade a tee party."

Annie gave up her sister for faking an illness. She stood up for truth and justice.

Out of the moths of babs.

From Riley's journal, dated April 24, 2005: "I had a sa pris. My Dad kam home arlay we had pancacs for brakst and then we went owt and wokt arawd the owtsid moll. My mom tot me how to fiye my shos. Riley."

Ms. Herlihy wrote, "You're growing up."

Finally, the truth.

I've taught the girls a few things, mostly irrelevant things. Things such as how to run pass routes in the family room, how to grip a football, how to read the *Daily Racing Form,* how to rub my ankle, how to throw wood on the fire without getting burned, how to light fireworks and run, how to sometimes skip a rock, how to jump off my shoulders into water, how to cheer for any team from Seattle, how to say "peek-a-boo" in Japanese, how to use Google Earth and pretend you are flying an airplane, how to pretend you are an airplane by sticking your arms out and making airplane noise, how to see faces in the moon, how to make bird calls to signal each other when sneaking up on Mom at the grocery store when she is shopping and we are just screwing around, how to hit the snooze button on the alarm clock, how to make sure to use the letter *t* when everyone else in Connecticut doesn't, how to play poker, Yahtzee, Scrabble, and casino craps, how to tap shrimp three times after dipping it in soy sauce so the soy sauce doesn't stain your clothes, how to say "Straight cash, homey" like Randy Moss, how to turn the TV on and off with the remote, and how to hit a balloon in the air as many times as possible without letting it hit the ground.

That's all fairly impressive, I know.

A little thing called parenting.

But there's one more thing I'll teach them for certain.

Don't cheat. Write your own story.

Like Riley's on March 4, 2005: "Today I had a 10 on behavyr. I wint and got hot coco. And then we wint home. Thin my dad kam hom. Riley."

Like Annie's on March 15, 2007: "My dad came home. I shawtid haray thin I sall my frend Morgan thin I boot a new book abawt the ender grend rall road."

Those are my daughters.

These are their pictures of me.

Cheater. Teacher.

I have too grat dawters. I lov them lik nothng els.

This chapter had too many topics for me to come up with a relevant fact as an end piece.

Controlled Scramble

This chapter's title is my preferred way of living life, and since this is almost a sports book, it was also the name of an old Seattle Seahawk play. At least I thought it was until I asked Jim Zorn, the perfect quarterback to pull it off, what the real name of the play was. He spit out several options and the whole thing was getting fairly confusing. Finally, I just told him, "Look. The name of the book has the words 'Incomplete' and 'Inaccurate' in it. Can I just go with what I've written?"

In the early days of the Seahawks, it was nearly a total scramble for Jim Zorn. He had an expansion team's offensive line, and he was constantly trying to come from behind. His ability to throw while on the run wasn't just an asset, it was a necessity. So they wrote up a play that matched his skill set: Controlled Scramble.

The look of the play was utter chaos: Zorn would sprint out in one direction while the receivers flowed to that side of the field. Then he would reverse course and drop back even deeper in a rollout to the opposite side of the field. Something like this.

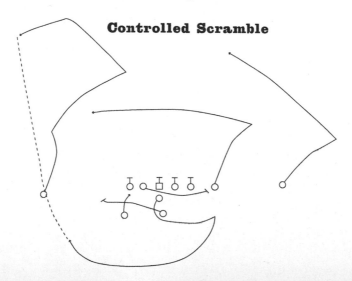

Controlled Scramble

By the time Zorn sprinted one way, then the other, he was a good twenty to twenty-five yards behind the line of scrimmage. (Normal rollouts have the quarterback eight to ten yards behind the line of scrimmage.) While Zorn was rolling right and then back to the left, his future Hall of Fame receiver Steve Largent was doing something similar. He'd open the play split left, run a deep post to the right, then turn himself around into a deep corner on the left (or sometimes break that into an "out" route).

The crowd (and the defense) would think they'd witnessed an incredible impromptu play. What they'd really seen was something else entirely: the *illusion of chaos.* Zorn and Largent knew where they were going all along.

In a perfect world, there'd be some great life lesson to offer up here. Something about being diligent in all you do (Controlled) while being a bit reckless in what you aim for (Scramble). Most of us aren't fortunate enough to be in a position to take such risks. There are bills to pay, mouths to feed.

It's emancipating once in a while to take a shot at the moon, even if convention would suggest you ought to stay grounded.

My controlled scramble happened in early 1994.

I'd been a freelance reporter for ESPN for four years or so, shortly after leaving a television job in Seattle. The network would call and ask me to get some player sound from one of the Seattle teams. I would send the tape but also write up a full story, my version of extra credit to impress the bosses.

Mostly, though, they saw me as a pest. One boss told his subordinates not to return my story pitch calls.

But they defied him. And in my mind kept the door open.

Finally, in early 1994, I had just about given up on getting hired full-time. I had been strung along (freelance reporters are actually called "stringers") for too long. It was time to try a bigger play. I sent the following note to John Walsh, the man in charge of editorial decisions at ESPN.

As you see, they checked the middle box, "keep doing what you're doing."

A month later I was hired.

March 4, 1994

Mr. John Walsh
ESPN
ESPN Plaza
Bristol, Connecticut 06010

Dear John:

Please mark the appropriate box and return as I am in the process of planning my future.

> **It just hit us -- we love your work. Contract is on the way.** ☐
> **Stand by the mailbox.**

> **Keep up the field producing. We'll call you when we need you.** ☑

> **We'll consider hiring you about the time ESPN5 hits the air.** ☐

Thanks,

[signature]

Kenny Mayne

25818 15th Avenue South
Kent, Washington 98032

(206)382-3995 (work)
(206)839-1537 (home)
(206)996-5975 (pager)

Kenny —

Keep up the good work!

— Jim Ebben

Here is a relevant fact about somebody mentioned in this "Controlled Scramble" chapter.

Steve Largent played his entire Hall of Fame career with the Seahawks but he was first drafted by the Houston Oilers in the fourth round of the 1976 draft. He was the nineteenth receiver chosen. I got to throw passes to him during my tryout with Seattle. He had good hands.

Dancing

Dancing is not a sport when all you're doing is staying an extra two hours after the junior high bell to stand around against the wall and debate for one hour and fifty minutes whether or not to ask Susan Nelson if she wants to take to the floor. Of course she wants to dance. She probably wanted to dance an hour and fifty minutes ago. She came to the stupid dance, in the stupid cafeteria, with the stupid teachers who stand around and make fun of the stupid kids who are afraid to dance, or the stupid kids who do dance. The music is blaring from the jukebox. (We really played the music from a jukebox.) The clock is ticking. There is only so much red punch a fourteen-year-old can drink.

And now it's time. The question is finally posed. And she does want to dance. But then Roberta Flack's "Killing Me Softly" plays and that means it's going to be a *slow dance.* How can somebody who is afraid of girls slow-dance? Why did I stay for this? I could be playing Wiffle ball right now. I could be cheating my grandma at Scrabble and biting the fat on her arms. But no. I'm standing there, frozen, and they are playing "Killing Me Softly."

Kill *me.* This sucks. Why didn't I pay attention during sixth-grade sex education? Something's supposed to be going on. The song ends. The dance ends. I hate dancing.

ABC calls and asks if I want to be on *Dancing with the Stars.* You mean I get to dance with Jessica Lange? Sure. How much does it pay?

I'm the star? What kind of lame show is this if I'm the star?

Right. I can't even get an invite to the ESPY Awards and I'm a star? Is there a worldwide shortage of stars? I call back and gain confirmation that they really are paying money for people like me to dance. I'm all for making a fool of myself. I do that for a living. But in those cases, I usually control the extent of the foolishness. This is an entirely different animal. They want me to dance *live* on television. I don't even like to dance. Hadn't the Susan Nelson–Roberta Flack story been on *Deadspin*?

There was a second question. Is Jerry Rice really doing this? They came back with confirmation on money and Rice, and all of a sudden I was a paid *professional dancer.*

They set me up with Andrea Hale, a pretty and pretty tall girl from Utah. Our first meeting was videotaped by the producer assigned to us so as to capture one of those *real moments* that aren't all that real in reality TV. I dipped her, I spun her. I almost tripped and fell down.

Andrea flew to Connecticut, where I live, so we could practice for three or four consecutive days before I had to fly off to do my real job for ESPN (it was tackle football season). I'd go do my story, then return to meet Andrea for another few days of practice. The cha-cha was our task.

I sucked.

I had a built-in excuse for any failure. On good days my right ankle is merely swollen. On bad days it is grotesque. This is from an old tackle football injury (see chapters on tackle football).

Andrea was quick to inform me that the cha-cha is more of a sliding and "striking the floor" dance; therefore my injured-ankle excuse wasn't going to fly.

So we worked. And worked. Sometimes we went for five straight hours. Sometimes we did that and came back for a few more hours in the evening. We practiced as though we were going to be on national TV and dance live before millions of people.

Killing me softly.

The producer shot every second of every practice so that when it came time to show the national audience how we had prepared, the show could use *all three examples* in our seventy hours together when Andrea got mad at me for screwing around. We actually got on famously, but the show, being a reality show, sought to display the most confrontational moments of our time together. "You've got to stop joking around" is how Andrea was seen putting it. So there, they had it. The audience saw the TV guy painted as a screw-off, the guy who couldn't care less about the show or his performance in it.

The real truth is I hadn't tried so hard at anything since the last days of my tackle football career a quarter century previous. I didn't take myself seriously, and knew I wasn't much of a dancer, but I took the mission very seriously. As bad a dancer as I was and still am, I didn't want to perform poorly. Whether it's Yahtzee with my wife or golf with my friends, I'd rather win than lose.

We would lose.

The night before our dance I attended maybe the greatest game in the history of college tackle football. Texas beat USC on a last-minute touchdown by Vince Young. I saw that part on TV. I was sitting fifty-yard line for the greatest game anyone can remember but *only for the first half.* I felt I needed to *beat the traffic, get to my hotel, and be rested for my big dance performance.*

This was the worst decision in the history of sports.

Before leaving I stumbled across Michael Jordan, who was good enough to give me and my NFL features producer, Tom McCollum, a short line on camera for the story we were working on that week. Jordan asked me, "Why are you doing it?" "What?" I asked in return. Then I knew. He was mocking me for taking the *Dancing with the Stars* role. I told him they were paying me. "It better be a lot," he said.

I informed Tom that I really needed to leave. He looked at me strangely. He looked at me like he was a guy who had just heard that his friend was going to *leave the Rose Bowl to get ready for an appearance on* Dancing with the Stars.

I'm supposed to apologize for being diligent?

I listened to the third quarter on the radio, saw the finish on my hotel TV.

I had a chance to get plenty of rest. Except that I didn't sleep at all. I didn't sleep at all because the next evening I was going to dance on national television. I'd rather be fourteen in the cafeteria. Susan Nelson no longer scared me. Who does Susan Nelson think she is?

Andrea and I stood apart on the floor to begin our cha-cha. She had a nervous smile on her face. I believe she was worried that I'd carry out my threat to abandon the routine if things went badly, just go Chris Farley on them. I told her when in doubt, I'd go for the laugh.

I didn't do that.

They laughed anyway.

The background story on our training finished up, the one about how I didn't care what was about to take place. Only I did care.

As a bonus, I remembered all my moves. They weren't elegant moves but I hit my marks.

My main goal was: *Do not drop Andrea.*

I almost did at the end. She has heavy thighs. But I did *not* drop the girl.

Before that, I did drop something. I intentionally waved off one of the moves I'd had trouble with in practice. I thought the judges and audience would find it amusing. I mean, I did get right back on our routine. Instead, they were collectively troubled by the throwaway. The guy who they thought didn't care about the program had demonstrated it right there for all to see.

What I was really trying to do was not ruin the entire routine for the sake of one two-second move. It had always been our toughest section in practice. So I blew it off.

I also waved to Jerry Rice's wife in the audience when I dipped Andrea. It seemed like the right thing to do at the time.

Andrea and I had debated whether the right approach was to do something quite easy that I might almost master, or something very difficult that would win us points for effort. We did nothing as difficult as Drew Lachey. He looked like he'd danced in ninth grade for sure. But compared with some of the others, we thought our routine was quite ambitious.

Then we found ourselves in last place. But that was the fans' choice. The judges had us in *second-to-last place.*

We finished our number, held hands, and walked toward the judges' stand. The Italian judge killed me right out of the gate. I don't recall exactly what he said.

(The editor does.)

Italian Judge: That was demented. It was like Pinocchio chasing Jiminy Cricket across the room. It couldn't have been more wooden.

The female judge mocked me with laughter. Only Len Goodman gave me any praise at all. Then he gave me a 5 on a scale of 10. Not exactly a full-fledged endorsement. The other two gave me a pair of 4s, a total of 13 on a 30 scale.

I felt bad for Andrea because she's a good dancer and deserved better. She impressed me with her loyalty. She defended me, told me I hit all my marks, said the Italian was a dork.

Andrea and I had held our comments when on stage. I turned away from the judges at one point and whispered to her, "Ignore them."

Andrea looked sad, in the way girls look sad sometimes.

Backstage, they gave me the microphone. "I don't think the Italian judge understood what we were trying to portray out there. We're supposed to be two children lost in the woods and there's a snowstorm and then the tanks are coming but you know we hide under the bridge and then we captured each other at the end, then we almost dropped a girl but she has fancy sequins, I picked her up, I'm married already, okay, and I'm just escorting her through the woods."

There was some laughter from the audience but mostly I remained the butt of the joke. A 13 out of 30.

You'd think one could have rolled around on the floor and received a higher score. We should have tried that. The next afternoon, a few hours before the cut-down show would start, a publicity representative from ABC asked me if I'd go on *Regis* in New York the next day if we were the first team to be eliminated. I asked her if that was already a known fact. She claimed she didn't know. We agreed to do the New York trip if we got the ax. New York City is always a good time.

It wasn't such a good time this time.

But then, L.A. had been kind of rough too.

We stood on the stage, all ten couples. One by one, Tom Bergeron and Samantha Harris announced the couples who were moving forward. "Ashly and Master P, you're moving to round two."

It was then that I said to Andrea and Drew Lachey (standing next to me): "We're dead."

Lachey said, "Shut up." He had been my next-door neighbor in the dressing room area. We had hit it off fairly well. We'd made great strides since the day I had confused him with his brother, Nick. I knew Drew was being kind but I also knew he was out of his mind.

George Hamilton and Jerry Rice had already been named as moving forward to the next round. There was no one else to cut *but us.* When Master P got the extension I should have just walked down to the floor with Andrea and checked out. At least that way I would have gotten the mic back one more time.

Instead they mistimed the show a bit and "crashed off," as the saying goes. Tom Bergeron hustled us away from the good-bye interview.

I protested with "I have more to say."

I tore off my dance shoes and threw them into the audience (it didn't make air). I tried to rip my shirt, but it was a sturdy shirt. That, or in addition to being a crappy dancer, I'm a weakling.

I went to my dressing room, called my wife. I got out of the dance costume and into civilian clothes. I talked with the line of entertainment reporters. I kissed Andrea good-bye. George Hamilton called it a travesty of justice. The talent coordinator who had first contacted me about doing the show told me, "Don't worry about this at all. ABC already has another show for you." (The show was killed in development, the definition of "development" being that phone calls take place.)

I took my nephew Jeff, niece Kendall, and friend Kan Mattoo out for some post–reality show commiseration.

For all I know Skybar isn't even considered cool any longer. But what do I know? I'm from Kent, Washington. Kendall and Jeff hadn't seen the place (an outdoor nightclub at the Mondrian Hotel on Sunset), and I was going to play connected uncle who would show the kids the town. Entrance to Skybar is achieved if (a) you are a guest of the Mondrian, (b) you are a hot girl without any guys in tow, (c) you are perceived as being cool by the guys in the camel-colored blazers at the door. I wasn't staying at the Mondrian on this trip, but I'd stayed there plenty and was known to a lot of the staff.

Most of those staff members were not working that night.

I did run into one bellman I knew. He said he'd get me on the list for Skybar.

This list was lost or stolen.

Guy in Camel-Colored Blazer: What can I do for you?
Me: Let us in?
Guy in Camel-Colored Blazer: Are you a guest of the hotel?
Me: Many times. But not this time.
Guy in Camel-Colored Blazer: Are you on the list?
Me: Yes. I believe I am.

The Guy in the Camel-Colored Blazer was in Skybar only because he worked there. He pretended to look over a list but it looked to me more like a stray piece of paper that had been left behind at the podium.

Guy in Camel-Colored Blazer: No. Sorry.

I looked back to my niece and nephew and threw up my hands. Kan laughed knowingly. He knows about this kind of stuff.

We huddled in the lobby of the hotel. We looked for the one bell-man who knew me. Plan B became another trendy or formerly trendy place down the street, Chateau Marmont.

The guy in the camel-colored blazer was a charmer compared with the crew who met us outside Chateau Marmont. In this case, we didn't get a foot onto the property. These important guys stopped us at the curb on Sunset.

Guy Who Would Not Let Us Step Past the Curb: Can I help you?
Me: Let us in?
Guy Who Would Not Let Us Step Past the Curb: No.
Me: Do you think we could get into 7-Eleven or International House of Pancakes?
Guy Who Would Not Let Us Step Past the Curb: Yeah. (Laughing, like he'd thought of it.) That's more your speed.
Me: I'll do the jokes.

My niece, nephew, and Kan then laughed at me. The loserhood of being first off on a reality show was starting to sink in.

Just then a lady approached.

Lady Who Approached: Kenny Mayne! Kenny Mayne! I love you! You were great on the show. I can't believe they threw you off so quick!
Me: That's kind of you.
Lady Who Approached: Can I get a picture with you?
Me: Sure.

The others laughed, as though this were a nice turn of fate. Somebody in this town had recognized me and actually liked me.

Lady Who Approached: Never mind. I don't have any film left in the camera.

We went bowling.

The bowling alley is across the street from where Jimmy Kimmel does his show. It was his taping hour. Jeff and I decided I should crash Kimmel's show and walk on just like Don Rickles used to do with Johnny Carson. I knew Kimmel would be okay with it. I had been on his show just a few days before. This was a perfect follow-up. Jimmy would make fun of me, but in a friendly, even funny way. This night could still end well.

As I was getting entrance at the backstage door, Jimmy's girlfriend, Sarah Silverman, walked up with a hug and a nice hello. But something seemed a bit odd about the way she addressed me.

Sarah (whispering, like she was telling me someone we knew had cancer): Kenny. Master P is on the show tonight. (Pause.) But you should come in.

As well as I got along with Master P, I saw this as a bad PR move. He had made it and been invited over. I had been eliminated and would be seen as stealing his time.

We went to the bowling alley. The lanes were full (apparently lots of people have four hundred dollars to go bowling with) at the trendy alley, so we began with food. A producer from Jimmy's show found me and told me it would be great if I made a joint appearance with Master P. I declined.

I don't get real mad real often. When I do, my best release is to throw something. A baseball against a wall, a Wiffle ball even.

I grabbed a sixteen-pound ball. I threw my arm out. The former tackle football player Terrell Davis was in the next lane. By now he must have told dozens of people how "Kenny Mayne sure can throw a bowling ball hard."

Or maybe, "That loser Kenny Mayne went *bowling* after being kicked off *Dancing with the Stars.*"

Andrea and I flew to New York in one of those fancy-time Boeing airplanes. Andrea had never seen first class before, so the flight attendant, when making the introductions of the stars in the in-flight movie, dropped in her name as a kind gesture.

New York, just like I pictured it, skyscrapers and everything. And at 8 a.m., a car service to the studio where Regis does his show.

When we arrived, something seemed queer. It felt like they viewed us as circus cousins who had just married on a reality show. I haven't done that many TV shows, but the treatment from Jimmy Kimmel's people, and Carson Daly's, and *Good Morning America*'s, was always warm. Even if I'm nothing more than some dork from Kent, Washington (and I am), on those occasions when I was the *guest* I was always made to feel like a special one.

The circus cousins were asked to go to the studio floor by one of the assistant producers. She seemed tense. We'd be right with her when we got to the floor.

I don't really know what Gelman looks like. But I think it was him. It was whoever was in charge, and Regis always says it's Gelman.

The guy who might have been Gelman then told us how we needed to dance for Regis.

Andrea and I had the same reaction, which was, *No!*

The guy who might have been Gelman and the girl who seemed tense told us how great it would be if we were to dance.

Andrea and I had the same reaction, which was still *no.* But this time, feeling the tenseness of the tense girl and the pressure of the guy who might have been Gelman, Andrea reasserted herself as my dance instructor. She tried to quickly make up a brief routine to our Donna Summer song that had served us so well in *Dancing with the Stars.*

I don't know why I went along, but for a few steps anyway, I did. We practiced our open once, then twice, at which point I called it quits. "If Joe Montana were your guest," I started in, "would you have him throw the football *left-handed*?"

I didn't get a big response from the guy who might have been Gelman or the girl who remained tense.

I tried to explain how I had done live television previously, how if Regis and Kelly threw some questions at me, I might be able to come up with an okay answer or two. I mentioned how they could show the clip from the *Dancing* show. I mentioned how their floor was not very big and how I had on regular street shoes and would likely trip over myself.

The guy who might have been Gelman said something about how "I know your work." He didn't say it in a way that inferred he liked my work. He wanted some kind of plan. He didn't like much the idea of just winging the segment. The girl who remained tense told us to "have fun with it."

As one of my ESPN photographers, Chuck Samataro, has pointed out, "have fun with it" is the television producer cop-out line for "I don't really have much of a plan here—please do something."

I didn't want to have fun with it, and I certainly wasn't having fun rehearsing for all the fun we could have.

Finally I stopped with the niceties, if that's what you could call what had transpired so far. "So let me get this straight," I started. "You want us to dance for sixty seconds, fail miserably, give Regis a terribly funny line to deliver, have him look smart, and have us look like complete asses? Is that what we're doing here?"

The guy who might have been Gelman said nothing. The girl who remained tense said even less, if that was possible.

We retired to our green room, where Andrea continued to try to work out a routine I could memorize in the next hour.

It was then that I fired Andrea as captain of our team. I told her the guests on a talk show don't have to do something if they're not comfortable with the plan. If Regis and the guy who might have been Gelman wanted to pay us what ABC had paid us, I'd have danced my ass off all show. But not for $835 (the AFTRA appearance fee). I told Andrea I was not going to dance. I told the girl who remained tense I would not dance. I told the girl who remained tense this very thing *each and every time she asked.*

Live with Regis and Kelly

Andrea and I were backstage now. *Fifteen seconds* before we were to go on stage, the girl who was now more tense than the last time she was referred to told us, hurriedly, that "plans have changed." She told us to go to the center of the stage; Regis and Kelly would start the *interview* from their side set position.

Andrea and I walked to our mark. I told her, "Follow me." I didn't think they would do what they did, but I didn't like where this was going. We took the floor and Regis said, "Here they are to do the cha-cha, Andrea and Kenny."

They played our Donna Summer song.

Andrea looked at me. I looked at her.

I gave the director the international *"cut the music"* sign with a slash to my throat. The music died.

Regis said, "Come on, Kenny, *dance*!!" I said: "If you like dancing so much, you dance."

I think they took a commercial after that.

We never sat down. We stood with Regis and Kelly and they said things talk show hosts say to people who just refused to go along with the producer's plan. Regis mentioned something about how it must have been rough finishing last place on the dancing show. "We don't look at it that way," I replied. "Right now we consider ourselves to be number ten in the world."

The show ended somehow. We walked backstage. The girl who

remained tense said, "The exit is around the corner." I told her I would be using it for the last time.

A few days later, a girl I know from *Good Morning America* e-mailed me and asked what exactly it was that went down on *Regis*. I explained the story and her reply was: "You should have danced for Regis. Regis *is* television."

There is every chance Regis didn't know about our refusal to dance. He might have been given some notes, or an outline as to how the show would play out.

Those last two sentences make me feel a lot better about television.

And dancing.

I do dance at weddings. Not well. Laura and I have a deal that if any Stevie Wonder plays or if the B-52s' "Love Shack" rolls, then I am required to dance. Other than that, dancing's chief role in my life remains playing *Dancing with the Stars* with my daughters on the family room floor. Our routines are tight. The judges are friendly. No one forces us to dance when we don't want to. We dance because we can.

It's in that place that there is no fear of dancing. I have the only audience I need.

I have fun with it.

Here is a relevant fact about dancing.

My score of 13 has some notable sporting companions. Wilt Chamberlain, Dan Marino, and Alex Rodriguez wore or wear number 13. Franco Harris was the 13th player taken in the 1972 NFL draft. He played for 13 seasons. The game-time temperature of "the Ice Bowl" was 13 degrees below zero.

One Thing About the Last Thing

I was rewriting the "Dancing" chapter on an airplane when suddenly my computer stopped working. Something about battery power.

Miracle upon miracles, all the material was saved for me in some kind of temporary hold file. I'm loving Microsoft right now.

Between the time I wrote what I thought had disappeared and I found out it had reappeared, I realized I had made a key error with regard to chronology. There is no way I could have been kicked off, disallowed from going to cool or formerly cool L.A. places, gone bowling, then met with Andrea to go to New York for *Regis* all in the same night. I now realize my mind somehow put the dance night, the kicked-off-show night, and my return-for-the-championship night (I think Stacy Kiebler got screwed) into some kind of overlapping time sequence. All the things happened. They just didn't necessarily happen in the order I suggested.

The thing about the *Regis* show is gospel.

You can't make me go back and start over on that whole dancing thing.

Here are Riley's and Anna's depictions of me on *Dancing with the Stars:*

I have no other relevant facts about dancing.

Time-out

Sideline Interview

Suzy Kolber: This is a critical time-out for you. You could lose a lot of readers if you don't come out big after the stoppage of play.

Me: I don't think people can actually take books back, can they? Nordstrom doesn't sell books, does it?

Suzy Kolber: So you're only interested in the money? Some authors would also be concerned about how their work is received.

Me: I'm an author?

Suzy Kolber: This is probably a good time for another of those illustrations by one of your daughters. I heard you sort of took them for a ride, as long as we're talking money.

Football
Riley Mayne

Me: They haven't had to pay for one meal their entire lives. I give them clothes, a roof over their head. Riley got an air horn for her bike just because she threw the ball from third all the way to first in a Little League game. I think they've been compensated just about enough.

Suzy: You proposed an indirect financial reward for your daughter excelling in a children's baseball game? Isn't the pressure of children's baseball already high enough without you adding a financial bonus element? I want out of this book.

Erin Andrews: What the hell? I'm new. I'll be a fictional character in the book.

Rachel Nichols: Me too!

Bill Pidto: What am I doing in this? This is a complete cruciate. Whadya have?

Me: Another picture?

Randy Moss

Dodgeball

Dodgeball enjoyed a resurgence when the movie of the same name was released in 2004, or whenever it was.

We called the game "soak 'em" in my phys ed classes. Whatever the name, this was the sport employed by the PE teacher when he wanted a break from teaching anything constructive. Or when he wanted twenty minutes free to walk down to the teacher's lounge and hit on the substitutes.

In dodgeball/soak 'em, players are divided into two teams and ordered to stay on their half of the court. The rules are somewhat varied, but as I know it, players are instructed to aim for the shoulders down when throwing a little red rubber ball at their classmates' *faces*.

If a player is hit with a ball, he or she is sent to the sideline. If a player catches a ball in the air, one of his or her teammates is allowed back into the game and the thrower is out. The game ends when all players on one side of the court have been hit in the face and no one is left on one side of the court. That, or when the PE teacher gets back from hitting on one of the substitutes.

The game is known chiefly for the devastating effect it had on underdeveloped seventh graders. Across from them were sneering eighth graders or larger seventh graders, some of them growing actual mustaches. With or without facial hair these sneering eighth graders or larger seventh graders showed an absolute disregard for the rules about "shoulders down" and drilled hapless underdeveloped seventh graders in the face with small red rubber balls.

The smarter underdeveloped seventh graders would stand about forty feet back of the center line, to minimize the pain of having a small red rubber ball planted on their temple. The cagier underdeveloped seventh grader would use another as a human shield. He would do this until he was the lone remaining player on his side. At this point his teammates would head for the showers and rinse with haste so as to avoid prolonged mocking from the sneering eighth graders with regard to the size of their penis. There was no point in staying on the sidelines, as there was very little, if any, chance that the underdeveloped seventh grader would somehow successfully catch the little red rubber ball and extend the game.

No point at all because the underdeveloped seventh grader was required by some kind of unwritten *Wimp Law* to now address the halfcourt line and stand in position to take his punishment. The overdeveloped sneering eighth graders would launch their entire arsenal. Welts were delivered. Game over.

Invariably none of these overdeveloped sneering eighth graders, macho as they seemed for twenty minutes, would amount to anything on any field of athletics by their junior year in high school.

Here is a relevant fact about dodgeball.

Official rules from the National Amateur Dodgeball Association (who knows about the pro rules?) dictate that six players are on a side, that a ball eight inches around and made of foam be used, and that the game last no longer than five minutes. There is no way any of my PE teachers could have closed the deal on the hot substitute teachers in five minutes, which explains why our games lasted the entire school period.

Duckpin Bowling

I have no idea how people play duckpin bowling.

> Here is a relevant fact about duckpin bowling.
>
> Baltimore, Maryland, is the birthplace of both duckpin bowling and Babe Ruth, who counted the game among his favorite sports next to baseball.

Still More
Duckpin Bowling

Maybe a month after I did the exhaustive research necessary to construct the preceding chapter, I received a phone call from an independent filmmaker. He wanted to use my voice for the narration of a documentary on duckpin bowling.

To quote Dave Barry, I am not making this part up.

I have no other relevant facts on duckpin bowling or Dave Barry.

Electric Tackle Football

The first tackle football game I purchased was through a mail-order advertisement in *Boys' Life,* if I'm not mistaken. If I'm mistaken then I'm wrong.

I had such high hopes. I would be playing a form of tackle football constantly with my pals. I was eight years old.

These were to be the greatest days of my life.

I carefully filled out the order form and inserted my twelve dollars (cash), and with my proud mother looking on, I licked and sealed the envelope, affixed a stamp, and sent this important communication on its way in our big silver mailbox up on South 272nd.

Each day for the next two weeks I stood by the mailbox as the day's mail was to be delivered. Each day I walked back down the driveway with nothing more important than the Sears bill.

That disappointment was nothing compared with what I suffered when the game finally arrived.

In my small mind I envisioned some kind of game in which tiny plastic football men would race around on a board made to look like a genuine tackle football field. I would design intricate passing plays for my tiny plastic football men and they would execute every detail.

I was going to be a tackle football genius before anyone had heard of Bill Walsh.

The game arrived one day. It was all board, no action. It came with a series of "play cards" for the offense and "play cards" for the defense. Each side was to make a play selection for the offense and formation for the defense. The result of the matchup was revealed by some kind of cheesy slide rule on the side of the low-rent playing field, and the spot of the ball would be changed.

These were supposed to have been the best days of my life.

I cried in the same way I would years later when algebra and geometry perplexed me. The eighth- and ninth-grade tears were due to the difficulty of the challenges I faced. The tears of an eight-year-old were due to my disappointment in this lame cardboard game that didn't challenge me in the least.

I'd thought I was going to receive some tiny plastic football player men and somehow they'd have something inside them that would allow them to run up and down the miniature field. Keep in mind, at the age of eight I also thought that my neighbor, Jeff Whidden, and I were capable of constructing a flying machine out of scrap two-by-fours. Jeff's plane had a far better shot at departure, since he didn't *nail his to the ground.*

It dawned on me that I had fallen for the sales pitch of the mail-order advertisement. I had been bamboozled. But it was my own fault. I should have known that no mail-order company, even in a country as great as ours, a country about to put a man on the moon, could really provide the technology to match the design going on in my head.

This is how that famous phrase was invented: We can put a man on the moon, but we can't send tiny plastic football men through the mail.

Not long after this disaster I learned of a great new invention. An American had created something called electric tackle football.

This game did not come in the mail. This game was purchased by my parents for me at Christmas.

SMALL CHILDREN WARNING: Small children should stop reading here. SANTA WILL NOT BRING YOU TOYS THIS CHRISTMAS IF YOU READ ANY OTHER MATERIAL BEFORE THE BOOK TELLS YOU TO.

(Some small children are wondering just how they'll know when it's lawful to begin reading again.)

GET AN OLDER PERSON TO READ FOR YOU.

I'd learned a few years earlier that Santa Claus is a controversial figure. It turns out it could be that parents wake up early on Christmas morning and put presents under the tree. Then they pretend that an obese man from the North Pole flies all night in a sleigh loaded with toys *for every good child in the world,* slides down the chimney, eats most of a cookie, and drinks some milk.

Right.

How did I believe all that in the first place? For that matter, once I learned Santa was this controversial, how did I believe that that mail-order company could send, for twelve dollars, tiny football player men who would execute my intricate passing offense? What would they eat? What would they do while I was at school?

I feel so stupid.

SMALL CHILDREN CAN READ AGAIN.

When I tore open the package, I couldn't believe my eyes. The game they called electric tackle football contained dozens of tiny football player men. With the flick of a button, they would execute my intricate passing offense.

These would be the greatest days of my life.

The rest of that year's Christmas gift haul was so insignificant that I can't recall a single other present. Who knows what Aunt Dixie purchased for me that year, or if she bought me anything. Who cares? I do know that when I saw *A Charlie Brown Christmas* for the first time, it was at Aunt Dixie's house. She lived down that long winding road above the field where I played my first ever tackle football game at age ten. You know the place.

If you were on my team.

Or if you are Aunt Dixie.

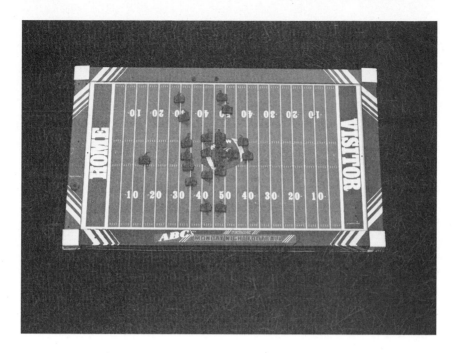

Last I checked, Aunt Dixie still thought I worked for C-SPAN. If she doesn't know where I work by now, how am I supposed to know what she got me in 1968, the year of Electric Tackle Football?

It turned out the tiny electric tackle football men couldn't really execute my intricate passing offense. This was mostly because it was nearly impossible to complete a pass. With the flick of an on-off switch, the tiny electric tackle football men would move around wildly on the vibrating aluminum electric tackle football field. On passing downs the player on offense was allowed to stop the action, place a small white felt football into the hand of the quarterback, pull back on the quarterback's plastic arm, and throw the ball to an open receiver, who was usually pointing in the wrong direction after having been vibrated out of his tiny plastic mind.

We didn't really read the rules to the game, just as my wife and I have never read the rules for any toy purchased for our children (or any appliance we have ever purchased). First of all, the electric tackle football quarterback who came with the game was about three times the size of the other tiny electric tackle football plastic men. It was a great height advantage for seeing over the line of scrimmage, but even a gullible eight-year-old such as me (so gullible that only months earlier I had believed a mail-order company could ship for twelve dollars dozens of tiny tackle football player men who could execute my intricate passing offense, watch TV with me, and sleep on small cots in my room) didn't really believe the quarterback or any of the tiny electric tackle football men could actually see.

With the quarterback dwarfing all others on the field, most of his passes went about five inches over the intended receiver's head. This taught me two important lessons. One, the key to success on the tackle football field is the establishment of a strong running game, and two, I needed to disregard the rules of electric tackle football, whatever the hell they were.

After several misguided throws by the extraordinarily tall quarterback, I put him on unconditional waivers and radically changed forever the game of electric tackle football. From that point forward, on all declared passing plays, one offensive player was removed from the field and the tiny white felt ball was placed on the soon-to-be vibrating aluminum field. This would be the spot of the "quarterback" for the intricate pass play that was about to unfold. If any defensive player crossed the imaginary line where the "quarterback" had been stationed, it would count as an official sack. Remember, the NFL didn't recognize sacks at this point in time. This is why Deacon Jones is so mad when you talk to him. My playing partners and I were years ahead of outdoor tackle football, though we didn't actually call it a sack. Somebody just yelled "Down!" when the player in passing formation fell asleep at the on-off switch.

When the electrical current was stopped on time, the player on offense would flick the tiny white felt ball down the field toward his open receiver. If the ball hit the receiver, it was a good catch, and the ball was placed in the receiver's arms, or on his plastic base in the case of receivers who'd been molded into a permanent blocking position. The receiver would then add yards after the catch, when the juice was turned back on and he could make forward progress until a defensive player's base made contact.

After about three hundred uses of this highly technical machinery, the electrical current would cease to run through the power cord. At this point electric tackle football was powered by the offensive player's fingers. With just the right touch an offensive player could tap on the aluminum tackle football field and cause the tiny plastic football men to move about just as they had done under electrical power.

I was the first environmentalist.

The game stayed in my possession for years. I cannot remember when I finally parted with the game, or when it parted with me. All I know is, electric tackle football, with or without the electricity, provided my most formative moments. Actually, I'm not sure about that. But I had already written "provided" and had to finish that sentence up big.

I would learn the tiny electric tackle football men weren't really up to executing my intricate passing offense, and in fact, they weren't really dependable for much of anything. They would run all over the field aimlessly, like kindergartners at recess. But once in a while I would find the Gale Sayers of electric tackle football. I would find the one tiny plastic football man who could run fast and *straight*. I would give him the ball over and over again. I would set up my tiny plastic football men in front of him and pound the ball left and right.

I was a genius before anyone had heard of Bill Walsh. The letdown of that day the mail-order company didn't deliver on its promise was long forgotten. These tiny plastic football men were durable and some of them dependable. They were always there, always waiting to play in their small plastic garbage bag that served as their locker room. Sure, sometimes they'd get mixed up and become hooked together by their arms and spin 'round and 'round. But mostly, they put forth an effort that replicated what the real players were doing inside the TV set in outdoor tackle football.

These tiny plastic football men provided fantasy before there was fantasy football.

They provided a childhood.

These were the greatest days of my life.

Years later I sought to buy my nephew Jeff his own electric tackle football game. I called every store in Seattle to find one. Most stores had never heard of the game. Finally, I called an 800 number for Sears.

Roebuck was long gone by then. The Sears representative told me they had *one* game left in the *country.*

One game.

I was purchasing the last electric tackle football game in America.

It didn't get to my house by Christmas Eve. It wasn't going to make it on time. I gave Jeff straight cash.

The game arrived a week later.

I still own it.

And now I have children. They were introduced to electric tackle football at a young age. Too young to understand the joys of hours spent lying supine on the family room rug, setting up players, keeping stats, being in the game.

We've put it away for a few years, a forgotten aluminum field that carries with it most of the best parts of the story of my childhood.

It's time to bring it back out, to line up the tiny plastic football men once more.

These will be the greatest days of our lives.

Here is a relevant fact about electric tackle football.

The game traces its roots back to 1929, which is weird because I didn't think they had electricity back then. Gamemaker Tudor began to offer prepainted plastic football men after Super Bowl I.

Fishing

In fishing, the angler digs a worm out of the ground, stabs it with a hook, and then releases enough fishing line so that the worm is now resting on the bottom of the lake. When this occurs, the following is probably what happens when two fish, what is called a *study group*, come upon the worm attached to the hook at the end of the fishing line at the bottom of the lake.

Fish #1: That looks like a worm.
Fish #2: That's odd.
Fish #1: I know. Worms usually thrive about six inches underground, in potato gardens.
Fish #2: Screw it. I'm hungry. Looks like a worm to me.

Fish #2 bites the worm, which lodges the hook in his mouth, which makes the bobber on the water go up and down violently in the water (but with nowhere near the violence of the experience of having a hook impale your cheek). This alerts a twelve-year-old boy to tug once, which makes the hook go through the face of Fish #2, at which point the twelve-year-old boy exclaims, "I got one!"

From there, the twelve-year-old boy works the reel clockwise to bring in the line, to bring up the fish, to take the hook out of the now flopping Fish #2's face, to try to grab the slimy Fish #2 in order to slap his head on the dock and kill him. At this point Fish #1 has something to say.

Fish #1: Jump back in the water!

The kid trips over the tackle box while trying to grab Fish #2, so as to slap his head on the dock and kill him. The fish goes flying out of the kid's hands, back into the water, with a small hole in his right cheek, but terribly glad to be alive.

Fish #2: I told you it was a worm!

Sometimes it doesn't work out even this well for the angler.

I grew up on Star Lake, south of Seattle. Legend has it a pilot flying above the lake named it Star Lake. I've flown above it, though I wasn't called a pilot. It looks like a bear claw you buy at the bakery. What kind of stupid name for a lake is Bear Claw Lake?

On fishing season's opening day in 1972, the Koszarek brothers, Joe and Al, came over with some other friends so we could all get our lines tangled together and kill some worms. Joe had an actual casting reel and fired out a tremendous amount of line with what seemed to the rest of us to be an expert casting technique.

Joe caught something right away.

It was a mallard.

A duck.

At this point, we were all greatly concerned for Joe, his fishing pole, with an actual casting reel, and the duck. So in unison, we laughed.

We did so for a good ten to fifteen minutes as the duck took off in the direction opposite the dock. The duck used up nearly every one of the three hundred feet of five-pound test weight line Joe had rigged up to his pole.

We were finally able to contain our laughter right about the time Joe's brother Al said, "Dad's going to kill Joe."

At this point, Al began to cry, even though it was Joe who was going to be killed. It was also right about this time when Joe lost his grip on the pole. The sudden weight shift added to the equation somehow dislodged the hook from the duck, who swam away, free at last.

The pole sank to the bottom of the lake, to be retrieved by a special twelve-year-old task force launched on the first day of seventy-five-degree weather that spring.

Joe ended up going to high school with me, so I know his father didn't really kill him. I haven't seen Joe since high school.

On that same dock years earlier, when I was five, I went fishing with my sisters on opening day. Some reels are made for casting, some are not. We held the cheapo noncasting kind, purchased the night before at Valu-Mart. A friend of my sister's tried to cast out her line anyway. Even if it had a casting mechanism, the pole would have broken in half had the girl extended her arm toward the lake. That's because the hook was now responsible for about fifty pounds of bait.

Me.

On her backswing she landed the hook in my right earlobe. I wanted to cry in the same way Al Koszarek cried the day he feared for his brother's life. But I'd been instructed over and again that I wasn't to make very much noise when fishing. It might scare away the fish, and the old-timers in the boats, the ones dressed for war and who owned much larger tackle boxes, might get cross.

So I held it in. I looked to my dad. He was about twenty yards away from me, smoking a cigar. He walked (*walked!*) out to the dock, yanked the hook out of my ear, and proceeded to kill a worm. My sister's friend was back in business.

These days, there are people who know how to fish without hooking little persons in the right earlobe, without catching ducks, and who own even larger tackle boxes than the old-timers dressed for war. These people make hundreds of thousands of dollars. They fish.

And you're not going to believe this part, but it's all on the TV.

You'll think I am, but I'm not lying when I tell you these people receive standing ovations when they bring the fish they have caught into arenas and hold them above their heads as though they are hoisting the Vince Lombardi Trophy.

It's so much more competitive than when I was a kid. When I was in ninth grade, whoever the guy was from whatever the government agency was that ruled over small lakes south of Seattle went out in a boat and dumped some kind of chemical into Star Lake to kill off a plant called milfoil. The weed was growing like a weed. It was making it dangerous to swim in certain parts of the lake, and my parents signed a petition so that the guy from whatever government agency it was that ruled over small lakes south of Seattle would come over and dump chemicals from a boat into our lake.

The chemicals killed the milfoil except for the milfoil that grew taller. But it definitely had a lot of killing power. It killed off the catfish.

They were ugly looking even before the guy from whatever government agency it was that ruled over small lakes south of Seattle dumped his chemical off a boat in our lake. But now the catfish had obtained a freaky-looking beard made of slime and fungus. It looked like a bunch of pollywogs had been attached to their faces. It also made them swim as though they were towing the boat driven by the guy from whatever government agency it was that ruled over small lakes south of Seattle.

For sport, or maybe because subconsciously we thought we were putting them out of their misery, but probably mostly for sport, we killed some of these slow-moving, slime-fungus-beard-wearing catfish. The theoretical sporting part of this exercise was that one of my neighbor friends, Jeff Whidden, had a father who owned a tackle box bigger than those of the men who dressed for war, but smaller than those owned by the fishermen who would later fish for hundreds of thousands of dollars. And he had a spear.

We were spear fishermen now. We went Kevorkian on the catfish. We speared to death some of the slow-moving slime-fungus-beard-wearing catfish.

When I look back now, so many years removed from the foolishness of youth, I can tell you, without reservation, it was fun as hell.

We must have speared dozens of those stupid catfish.

We didn't kill any worms in the process. You can say that for us.

Forty years later, Star Lake still has milfoil.

Can't speak for the catfish.

Here is a relevant fact about fishing.

Although freshwater lakes and rivers constitute less than .001 percent of the total volume of water on earth, 40 percent of fish species are found there.

Fishing: Now I Get It

Now I see why people are on their feet when a guy enters a room holding up a seven-pound largemouth bass.

By the way, "a guy" is more accurately described as "an angler." The guys who get up early to fish desire to be called "anglers" much in the same way Tour professionals insist on being called "players" rather than "golfers." It's sort of like how left tackles in tackle football want to be called "left tackles" as opposed to "fat guys who hold a lot and cannot always remember the snap count."

But here's why I get it now. Back in 1995, I was hauled into the boss's office at ESPN. This was the actual conversation.

Boss: Do you know anything about car racing?
Me: Nothing. Nothing at all.
Boss: Good. You're the new host of the new car-racing show.

It made me wonder what the first guy who was offered the job had said.

First Guy Offered the Job: I know nothing about car racing but
  I do know that you are a fat bastard.

So I was the car-racing show's host. I remember being devastated by the news. I guess I hadn't read up on how NASCAR was the run-away leader in the category of fastest-growing American sport. Stuart Scott (who loves electric tackle football too) had been given the new NBA show. Bill Pidto was assigned to *NFL Primetime*, the most important show in the history of sports television. Long live *NFL Primetime*. (Chris Berman, the godfather of ESPN, and Tom Jackson hosted *Primetime* for eighteen years before it was canceled when NBC took over *Sunday Night Tackle Football*.) All my col-leagues were doing all those cool things, and I was being sent off to cover car racing.

But then I went to the Daytona 500.

And then I gave thanks to the guy who must have called the boss a fat bastard.

Same deal in February of 2007. This time I sort of knew bass fish-ing was a big damn deal. At the same time, I knew the event I was to cover wasn't exactly NBA All-Star Weekend.

But then I went out on the lake, about an hour outside Birming-ham, Alabama. A guy named Tripp powered me and my cameraman and producer at speeds upwards of 70 mph.

The next time I tell the story it will be 80 mph.

We were doing about 110 mph on Lay Lake, looking for anglers.

The BASS Masters Classic was just a couple days off. This would be the final practice session for the fifty competitors. My assignment was to create a feature story for ESPN's BASS programming (which would also run on *SportsCenter*) and to host a banquet in honor of the best in BASS from 2006 and the new crop of elite anglers for 2007.

As I flew to Birmingham, I did not know the name of one angler. In fact, I thought whatever their names would turn out to be, they were called fishermen.

Tripp and the others corrected me on that. And like that virginal experience at the Daytona 500, they also blew me away with what it is they do that makes an audience stand in ovation when an *angler* arrives at the arena holding a seven-pound largemouth bass over his head.

It's not at all like when Joe Koszarek caught a duck. It's a galaxy removed from the days when on the night before opening day I would go with my dad to Valu-Mart to buy a twelve-dollar pole. They don't even call them poles anymore. I think they are now re-ferred to as rods.

The *anglers* bring with them ten rods. This is very smart because oftentimes the Valu-Mart poles would snap in half at the sight of a one-pound catfish.

The *anglers* don't just hop in the boat, crack open a beer, and stuff in a big wad of chew as they drop their lines into the water. Matter of fact, I didn't see anyone with a beer. It was as though BASS and AA had merged.

The *anglers* have sonar on board, and average-temperature charts, and forty different kinds of bait for their ten different rods. They don't dress like they're going to war. They wear bodysuits Terrell Owens would be proud of, with more sponsorship patches than are affixed to Jeff Gordon's fire suit.

Again, these guys *fish for a living.* They have tricked Toyota and Purolator and every company associated with everything there is with regard to *angling* into paying them money to drive around in speedboats at 200 mph. And they get as much as five hundred thou-sand dollars for catching the biggest fish on certain weekends.

I told them at the banquet that if "I found a way to get paid to fish for a living, I would hold a banquet too."

That was supposed to be a compliment.

No one laughed.

Maybe that's because the *anglers* already know how good they've got it. And how many people will fill arenas to stand in ovation when an *angler* holds a seven-pound largemouth bass above his head.

The joke was on me for not getting it sooner.

I have no other relevant facts about fishing. But I do have one other story. Once, when my nephew Troy (who is blind) and I were going fishing, I stopped at a grocery store and bought a trout. I hooked it onto his line and dropped it in the water and told him to reel it in: "You have a big one."

This next part is true. Polygraph tests are a fixture in competitive fishing tournaments.

Two-Minute Warning Before the Half

The book probably isn't going to get any better.

Flying

Even before Ben Stiller killed that airline counter computer scene in *Meet the Parents,* I had always wondered why airline check-in counter employees madly type in so many characters on their keyboards when the question from the customer is often nothing more complicated than "Can I have seat 11C instead of 12F?"

My dad worked for thirty-five years at the United Airlines counter at Sea-Tac Airport, south of Seattle. My sisters and I called it "Dad's airport."

We still do.

There's a chance the airline check-in counter employees are typing nothing more than xlwhyedlh35u33 **9((+−0_7 3 529 boat. As long as that gets me 11C I don't really care.

Back in my dad's day, airline check-in counter employees didn't have to type nonsense into their computers. In fact, they didn't have computers. They had green felt pens.

(I know there is a comic who did this bit on an HBO special, but I swear I was thinking the same thing at age seven, even before I knew what a computer was.)

My father's gone now and we receive no lifetime benefits from United. Those three-dollar trips to Hawaii were a good deal. So were the six-dollar trips when first class was open. So I think I'm safe from a legal and moral standpoint to admit now that my father used every bit of the discretion vested in him to upgrade old ladies, ex–football coaches of mine, and friends of the family with the *stroke of a green felt pen.* He would just mark the boarding pass with "2B" and the plane would take off. Air travel was more glamorous back then.

His marking up of coach-class boarding passes can't possibly be the reason United has struggled so mightily over the years. I mean, the seats were open. The first-class meals were already cooked, the real linen napkins already folded.

For that matter, out of loyalty, I bought United stock on September *12*.

Point is, since my father's time at the counter in Seattle, things have changed.

For the worse.

It's not the necessary security-line procedures that bother me. (Though any time I see a five-year-old being wanded I don't feel any safer. It means there's one fewer wand for a bad guy.) What's troubling is the manner in which the passengers proceed through it. There's an excessive and unnecessary amount of tension in the security line that carries over to the boarding process.

There are your professional travelers, many of whom let it be known in posture and speech that they are professional travelers, and then there are your handful who either have never traveled since the security procedures were heightened or are simply as dumb as a piece of Samsonite luggage. They do need to be moved along a bit. But the rest of us? We are just standing there. Standing in a line.

So then, there really is no need to get anxious when the guy in front of you is pulling out his computer, taking off his shoes, or grabbing his clear plastic bag containing shampoo measuring 3.5 ounces or less.

If you are standing behind that person, it is your turn *when he is done.* There's no need to press up against him. No need to become impatient. You are next. After he is done.

Same for the boarding process. Unless you intend to long-jump over the head of the man in front of you to get to 54G, there's no getting past him, and no one will be getting by you, until he's had his chance to stow his belongings in the overhead bin, take off his jacket, place his newspaper in the seat pocket, place his copy of *Maxim* (cover down) on the seat, and then attempt to squeeze his 258 pounds into the four inches of passenger space left for him by the guy directly in front of him, who is in full recline.

It is at that point that *you can move forward* to 54G and watch as the rest of the passengers behind the next guy who is now first in line look at their watches, grimace, and await their coveted turn to be the next guy to be first in line.

The following should be printed as an addendum to the Warsaw Convention stipulations that are found on the back of tickets:

NO ONE CAN BE THE NEXT PERSON TO BE THE FIRST PERSON IN LINE UNTIL THE LAST PERSON WHO WAS THE FIRST PERSON IN LINE IS SEATED. IT DOES NOT MATTER IF THE PERSON WHO IS THE FIRST PERSON IN LINE TAKES FIVE SECONDS OR FIVE MINUTES. YOU WILL NOT BE THE NEXT PERSON TO BE THE FIRST PERSON IN LINE UNTIL THE LAST PERSON TO BE THE FIRST PERSON IN LINE HAS BEEN SEATED.

And this isn't the worst of it.

The worst is Business Guy Who Usually Has a Large Blue Plastic Cellular Telephone Device Affixed to His Ear. He's the one who, upon taking his seat, makes a big production of the fact that he's not flying in first class, announcing to all (and whoever has to suffer through his cell phone connection) that "this is absolutely ridiculous! All these frequent-flier moochers are sitting up there and *I'm* riding in the back! I'm going to fire the bitch in travel. Whore."

Then it gets worse.

Business Guy Who Usually Has a Large Blue Plastic Cellular Telephone Device Affixed to His Ear: Yeah. Yeah. Just close the deal. (Pause.) No. You listen to me. I want this finished by COB. (Shorter pause, nowhere near long enough for the other passengers.) It's fifty-five K, pal. Now work it. (Pause.) These SOBs don't know what they're talking about. (Shorter pause, way too short now for the other passengers who wish the connection would fail.) Am I crazy? Am I crazy? [No.

You're a dork.] Tell Robson that if it's not finished by COB his ass is on the line. You feel me? [No. We hate you.] Good. I'll call you when I land. [Oh. Please do.] Let's do this thing.

Me: Please somebody make him shut up.

Business Guy Who Usually Has a Large Blue Plastic Cellular Telephone Device Affixed to His Ear: Somebody make the guy in 15D move his seat forward.

15D never does. In fact, he finds another button and spends the four-hour flight on 16D's lap.

Justice.

16D, the Business Guy Who Usually Has a Large Blue Plastic Cellular Telephone Device Affixed to His Ear, is also likely the same kind of guy my friend Scott Harves calls a "creeper." Creepers are the ones who close in on the jetway entrance area well before even the initial group of boarders (families with small children and the disabled) are called forward by the passenger agent who earlier in the day typed things such as c8ldhdlcnklh$$^^&ga_ into his keyboard at the front counter. Just after families with small children go down the jetway, airlines usually board first-class passengers, Super-Duper Flying Club members, and anyone who acts dumb enough to have not understood the boarding process.

The creepers block the entrance, forcing passengers who have actually been called to inquire of the creepers whether they are going forward or not. It creates one more unnecessary layer of tension in the already unnecessarily tension-filled process. Creepers, of course, lead the league in negative body language. They glare at Guy Who Is Now First in Line, who struggles by with his computer bag, duffel bag, and Jed Clampett paper bag filled with three weeks of old newspapers. That is, me.

For those who wasted the money, or fooled their companies into flying them first-class, the creepers also create an awkward situation in which Guy Who Has Either Wasted Money or Fooled His Company into Flying Him First-Class has to ask the creeper if he is flying in first class.

Guy Who Has Either Wasted Money or Fooled His Company into Flying Him First-Class (to creeper, who is blocking the entrance): Are you in first?
Creeper: Piss off.

Other than all of the above, airplanes are a marvelous invention and we shouldn't complain when the one we are flying on is twelve minutes late when we can't make it across town on time for a dentist appointment set six months ago.

Airplanes transport our favorite athletic stars around the globe so that we can watch them play sports.

This sentence was included so as to mention sports in a sports book and therefore keep this book on the sports shelf as opposed to the transportation shelf, a shelf no one buys anything off of, unless he is interested in the history of trains, which is, by the way, a pretty good read.

> I have one relevant sports fact about flying.
>
> One June 8, 1934, the Cincinnati GM Larry MacPhail flew nineteen of his players to Chicago for a series with the Cubs, making the Reds the first team to travel to a game by airplane. Twelve years later, the Yankees became the first team to fly on a regular basis.

Golf, Holes in One

If you ever hit more than one hole in one, they would be called holes in one, not hole in ones.

I've never hit one hole in one.

Noel Sansaver has five.

If it's in the paper, it must be true.

His holes in one were.

Noel is Mark Sansaver's older brother. One of them anyway. There are ten kids. Or there were. They are all grown now. You may have heard of Mark Sansaver. He broke Babe Ruth's home run record. (See "Wiffle Ball.")

Noel gained his fame less legitimately. And I was in on this.

It began with the one phone we had in our house growing up. Most of the time, my sisters monopolized *the one phone we had growing up*. No cell phones, no pagers, no Internet. Just one phone. One TV too. When we first moved in we actually had to *share the phone with the neighbors*. It was called a "party line." Some party. If we wanted to make a call, we had to check first to see if the neighbor wasn't already on the line. Usually they would (or we would) hasten the call to allow the other party to make theirs. Party on.

Once we acquired our own phone line—what a day that was—I was free to make fraudulent calls without the neighbors knowing about it.

There was the common stuff, ordering pizza deliveries to strangers' homes, calling up stores to ask if they had Prince Albert in a can (then let him out), and the ever popular call to a family name found in a phone book. You would call three times and ask for the name of a person who didn't live there. Each time, they'd say, "He doesn't live here." Then you would call back *as that person* and ask, "Have I had any phone calls?"

This was child's play, even though I was a child, maybe ten.

At that point my communication skills were ready to take on a new enterprise: I became KJR Radio, channel 95, AM.

KJR ran something called the "Cash Call Jackpot." A cash prize was on the line for any caller who could correctly identify the current cash prize amount (it grew each day when no one had the correct answer). The way it really worked was that KJR would take the tenth caller, or whatever caller number the DJ suggested. Since no one was calling my radio station, I made the calls.

Out of the phone book I'd grab a name and dial.

Me: This is Pat O'Day from KJR Radio. . . . It's time to Play Cash Call Jackpot, are you ready?

Gullible Person Who Could Not Distinguish the Voice of a Ten-Year-Old from a Disc Jockey's: Sure!

Me: Okay. The total is between three hundred and four hundred dollars.

Gullible Person Who Could Not Distinguish the Voice of a Ten-Year-Old from a Disc Jockey's: Three eighty-five?

Me: Did you say three ninety-five?

Gullible Person Who Could Not Distinguish the Voice of a Ten-Year-Old from a Disc Jockey's and Who Was Just About to Lie: Yes.

Me: I'm sorry. It was three eighty-five.

I learned a lot about people through this. They'll do anything for money.

Later, I learned the Seattle newspapers were understaffed. There was no one to check facts.

The Sansavers were from Wolf Point, Montana. After giving

Seattle a try for a number of years, several of the Sansavers moved back home to Montana.

Whenever Noel made a visit back to Seattle, he got his name in the paper.

By now I was in college, but still working on my communication skills. I would put on my "old guy who works at the pro shop" voice and call either of the Seattle papers and make up a tall tale about how "Noel Sansaver aced number 14. He was using a 9-iron, 128 yards. We're real happy for the young man."

Once I was out of school and in television, it would have been wrong for me to continue perpetrating this fraud on my hometown papers.

So I moved operations overseas.

At the height of the antiapartheid protests against South Africa, I was moved to do the following: go out for beers with my friend Jerry Hanley until midnight, watch the end of *Letterman,* and make this call:

> **Me (to the *Johannesburg Star*):** Yes. This is Art Arforder up here in Seattle. Your man Gary Player had quite a day.
> **Star:** Oh really. I know he's in the seniors tournament up that way.
> **Me:** Yes. He did quite well. Didn't win it. But the story got more interesting afterward. He challenged Gay Brewer to a sudden-death hole-by-hole match for ten thousand dollars. Quite a spectacle. And Player won it in three holes. Par, par, birdie. Amazing. The crowd ate it up. We just thought you might want to put a little note in your paper, being that Gary is from South Africa and all.

I then called the European news agency, Visnews, in London and claimed responsibility for the "fraudulent news reporting to the *Star* in South Africa on behalf of the Northwest Coalition Against Apartheid."

This is sort of like my Truth and Reconciliation.

More facts.

Tiger Woods hit a hole in one at age six. John Elway hit one on his fortieth birthday. *Golf Digest* says the average golfer needs twelve thousand shots to hit a hole in one.

Golf, Miniature

There are two kinds of miniature golf. There's the Disneyland kind, in which each hole has a magical setting, alluring in its extravagance to both child and adult alike. The artistry of the layout is splendid, the play is challenging yet entertaining.

The other kind of miniature golf is that which offers the patron a rusted-out clown's mouth and pond water so toxic the area is listed as an EPA Superfund cleanup site.

It's usually the latter variety that your six- and seven-year-old daughters want to play. While the older girl is diligent, setting up a four-inch putt with methodical care that by comparison would make it seem Sergio Garcia is involved in speed golf, the younger daughter disappears from view like a stray dog, only to be found bathing her doll or herself waste deep in the pond EPA officials in lab coats are testing.

> **Me:** Annie. I told you *not to touch the water*!
> **Annie:** I'm not. It's touching me.

The game ends when the clown's mouth of hole number 18 accepts the final shot of our round. There's no getting the ball back. It would be too risky to try to retrieve it.

So why is Annie on her belly, crawling under the rusted mesh-wire fence in an attempt to recover her powder blue golf ball?

> **Me:** Annie. What are you doing? I told you not to go near the rusted mesh-wire fencing!

Annie: I'm not. It's on top of me.

And now both girls have to go pee. We head to the "family" restroom. It's just like a Ritz-Carlton. A Ritz-Carlton that's downwind from a nuclear power accident site.

Me: Annie. Don't touch *anything.* I'll hold you above the seat. The sink is too dirty to wash your hands. Let's go to a bowling alley to clean up.

Here is an interesting and somewhat relevant fact about miniature golf.
   The first outdoor miniature golf courses in the United States were built on rooftops in New York City in 1926.

Golf, Other

I think it was Janeane Garofalo, or at least I know it was a girl any-way. I'm sure it was somebody funny on HBO who once said of golf: "It is men in pants, walking."

I love golf but I don't like it when those in charge make me wear pants.

I was allowed to play historic Winged Foot, outside New York City, a couple of times. These were charity events for the Special Olympics. The folks who paid money to support the cause had the high privilege of playing golf with people such as me. After two years of this, and I assume many complaints from the people stuck with playing with people such as me, the organizers changed the rules. From then on the people who were stuck playing golf with people such as me were allowed to play golf with people who could actually golf. Club pros were brought in to replace the *celebrities.* The celebri-ties, for the most part, are the ones who can best afford to pay money to play in such events and support the cause, but for some reason they are instead flown first-class and treated like they're somebody, so that people who are considered less a somebody can pay a bunch of money to get stuck playing golf with *celebrities* who can't golf well but are considered *celebrities.*

Back when the Winged Foot tournament was allowing people such as me to play the part of people other people would want to golf with, there was one particularly scorching summer day in which people didn't want to play with any people, even people Winged Foot thought would be people other people would want to play with. Peo-ple didn't want to play at all. Not with people. Not with themselves.

It was, give or take, three hundred degrees outside. Humidity was through the roof, and it felt like we were playing under one, us people. The roof of a greenhouse. It was miserable. And the people in charge at Winged Foot made all people, even people other people might have wanted to golf with, *wear long pants.*

For some reason, women were allowed to wear shorts. But no one was allowed to drive in golf carts, pants or no pants. We walked. We walked eighteen miserable holes at this beautiful golf course where people had paid a lot of money to golf with people other people thought people would want to be miserable with.

I drank, roughly, ten gallons of water, give or take the Central Park Reservoir. I crawled from miserable shot to miserable shot. The glory of the great old stone clubhouse, a clubhouse so great I sat in a chair for an hour before going out, to simply soak in the ambience, the glory of whatever I was just talking about didn't matter one iota when I was playing out the string after *the first hole.* From there, I could look back and see the clubhouse. I wished I was in it. In its shower. Or just sitting in any room that had air-conditioning. But instead, I soldiered on, one miserable shot after another. I turned in a scorecard with a number that looked like the temperature. It read 113.

None of this is a knock on Winged Foot. It is a glorious place. It's where the term "mulligan" was invented. Some guy from Canada with the last name Mulligan used to take extra shots when he felt like it. He joined Winged Foot and other people started copying his rule about taking extra shots when the time seemed right. Usually after a bad shot.

Winged Foot has other, more conventional rules. They are rules handed down for centuries, I suppose.

That's because when golf was invented, there were no electric carts.

If I remember correctly, and who cares if I don't, the game of golf was invented in Scotland. This happened a long time ago. Some Scottish people were tired of fighting the English or the Celts or whoever else was seeking a fight (maybe a JV game with France now and then). One day one of the Scots was talking to some other Scots.

The Scot Who Was Talking: What do you say we go walk around and hit a ball with a stick?

Scot Whose Successors Would Later Handle My Starbucks Order [see "Hunting"]: Huh?

The Scot Who Was Talking: And we'll keep hitting the ball, which jai alai players call a pelota, with the stick until we get close to a hole in the ground. Then we'll take a different stick and hit the ball softer so that it goes into the hole in the ground.

Scot Whose Successors Would Later Handle My Starbucks Order: That sounds good. I'll bring coffee and two more people so we can have a foursome.

After this conversation the four Scots thought it was so much fun to hit a ball with a stick and then with another stick, but softer, until the ball went into a hole in the ground, they decided to do the same thing another seventeen times. Thereafter, they did this eighteen times each time, except on those occasions when they felt like executives, in which case they did it nine times, hence the name "executive nine."

That's pretty much the story of golf's origin except that England beat Scotland at some point in war or something and took over the game of golf. The royal family may have then taken over because the body that rules golf, I think, is called the Royal and Ancients. How ancient can they be these days if they are still alive? Do they just take the oldest living people in England and put them in charge? Are these ancients the people I can go to if I want to wear shorts when it is three hundred degrees at Winged Foot? What if I want to change the game's rules so that we have to play only five holes and I can then get home in time to help my wife if I've been out of town a lot recently and don't want to feel guilty about not doing my part fixing stuff around the home even though the only things in my toolbox are a hammer and a screwdriver and sometimes a saw when I haven't lost it? Why can't golf be just five holes, especially when it's three hundred degrees and we're in long pants in a greenhouse?

In the name of full disclosure I should point out that I did some advertising work for Top Flite and its D-2 golf balls. These balls go the distance. I thought it would be wrong to mention Top Flite as many times as I have throughout the story about golf's origins without fully disclosing my relationship with Top Flite. Top Flite also makes golf clubs but I think they are called Callaway golf clubs. In some of these sentences, depending on how the good people at my publisher put the book together, the words Top Flite match up just about perfectly with the very next mention of the golf-equipment company I work for, Top Flite. I think I just missed right there as far as lining up Top Flite with Top Flite. Let   me   try   again   to   do   Top Flite. I may have done it right there but let me try again. Top Flite.

Top Flite.

Why did they spell Top Flite Top Flite instead of Top Flight? Was the name already taken? Top Flight, spelled that way, conjures up an image of flying. I have a chapter on flying. There's also a chapter on controlled scramble, which my agent says is my worst. But he hasn't seen this chapter.

Tiger Woods.

Here is a relevant fact about golf.

According to Forbes.com, Tiger Woods's caddie, Steve Williams, earned $1.27 million from June 2006 to June 2007. Had he been a tour player his earnings would have ranked him in the world's top seventy-five. But he's not a player. He's the guy who carries Tiger's clubs and yells at people to stop taking pictures of Tiger.

Halftime

It is half time. Or it's halftime. I always forget if that's one word or two. Who cares?

It's time to reflect on what's occurred so far. Not much really. At this point, it could be you are pissed you spent so much money on such a pile of nonsense. You might want to try to take it back to Nordstrom. Nordstrom takes back anything. The story goes that a long time ago, somebody took a used tire back to Nordstrom even though Nordstrom doesn't sell new tires.

Nordstrom is proud of this story. It's proof the store will do anything for the customer.

Remember the Susan Nelson girl mentioned three or four times earlier? I think she works for Nordstrom. Take the book to her.

This book was printed on used tires.

Enjoy halftime.

And enjoy half time.

The Stanford band is on the field.

Horse Racing

Horse racing is the second-greatest sport next to tackle football and everyone knows this.

My first recollection of horse racing was the Kentucky Derby of 1968. One horse, Dancer's Image, won the actual running of the race but another horse, Forward Pass, was later named the official winner. This had something to do with either drugs or racism. It's a long story, too long to be chronicled right here.

I believe it was the next year when my mother took me out to the track. The track was called Longacres, located in Tukwila, Washington, about ten miles south of Seattle, and ten miles north of where I grew up.

I won money on my first ever bet. Some people say it's bad to win on your first bet because it means you'll keep going back. Screw those people, I just won $2,700 betting Saratoga's opening day of the 2007 season.

After winning with my mom I returned to Longacres mostly with my uncle Gordy (and later, more habitually, with my friend Shawn Doran, and others from my high school, including the late Steve Derum and Dale Spencer, who famously bet fifty dollars on a single race in 1975).

Before the state government allowed us to drive (because twelve-year-olds don't often have wallets, where would we have stored our licenses?), Shawn and I used to hitchhike to the races. These were different times than today. I would never allow my daughters to hitchhike to the races. What kind of reckless, inattentive parenting would that be? There aren't even any Thoroughbred racetracks in the state of Connecticut. There's no way Riley and Annie could hitchhike back and forth to Belmont Park and be home in time for their baths.

My dad was fairly conservative regarding finances. He liked to play a twenty-dollar show parlay. That's a method of betting in which you start with your base amount (twenty in his case) and continue to play the base capital and all of your winnings on each subsequent race. My friends and I still run a show parlay when we get together for big events such as the Kentucky Derby or the Breeders' Cup. It rarely succeeds, but we earn the opportunity to talk about my dad.

My uncle Gordy was quite a bit less inhibited when it came to his gaming choices. In fact, he'd have let me hitchhike to any track in any state as long as I studied the *Daily Racing Form* with great diligence. He liked to bet twenty dollars too. But always to *win*. And he'd do so on horses whose odds were 30– and 40–1.

Gordo taught me lessons about risk and reward long before I heard trainer Nick Zito say, "You can't even *lose* if you don't enter." That is to say, you have to be in the game to have a chance at winning. It applies in all arenas. There'll be days when the 30– and 40–1 horses don't come home first, but when they do, the reward will have been worth the risk.

Gordy was an attorney by trade, but in some kind of queer business deal he ended up owning a laundry in Kent, Washington. By the time I was in high school, Shawn; another friend, Otis Embree; and I worked for Gordy part-time at the cleaners. The place was called Kent Norge, which allowed Otis to so easily create the Norge American Soccer League (named after the North American Soccer League) behind the front counter. There weren't all that many customers, so about 90 percent of the time Otis and I worked the night shift, we held NASL games with a Nerf ball behind the front counter.

Gordo would publish company newsletters, part exaggeration, part total fiction. If I hadn't lost them all I would print one right now. I feel as stupid as anyone who has ever misplaced a Honus Wagner baseball card.

Norge soccer was great but the best times came on weekends. A typical Saturday consisted of a 9 a.m. call time, two hours of mopping floors, cleaning out lint from the dryers, and filling the pop machines with cans of Coke (*not* Pepsi). We'd then take in a late breakfast and a *Daily Racing Form* study hall at the Coachman Restaurant next door. Then it was time. Gordo would fire up his Monte Carlo (what a fancy car, we thought), balance a cup of hot black coffee in one hand, and steer with the other down the West Valley Highway. I'd ride shotgun to his right, and sometimes he'd let me steer. Always, we used the ten-minute drive to revel in anticipation of the beautiful racetrack that awaited us and the untold riches that were ours for the taking.

With a glance over my right shoulder, I could see Mount Rainier in the distance. It's a fourteen-thousand-foot volcano that sits about two hours south of Seattle by car. (Once we were at the track, the view was dead on, just above the tall trees that encircled the south parking lot.)

It's a sight that makes me believe in God.

I'd read the *Form* stats to Gordy during the drive. He'd then interrupt with one of his long and intricate jokes. He repeated the same jokes more often than our total number of visits to Longacres, which is to say, a large number of times.

In one, a man is losing lots and lots of money at the racetrack. He is down to his last ten dollars. He places it on a horse whose odds to win are 100–1. If he wins, he's even for the season—all his money is back. He prays to God that if he can get a little help, he'll give half to the church. He'll even go to church. He'll treat his wife and children better. He'll be a good person.

When the horses hit the far turn his horse is dead last. The man starts praying even harder, making even bigger promises to God.

Suddenly, the horse begins to make a great rally on the far outside, picking off horses one by one. With a sixteenth of a mile to run, his horse takes the lead, then begins to pull away.

The man says, "I got it from here, God."

I could hear that story another ten thousand times, sitting in Gordo's Monte Carlo (what a fancy car) or sitting in a box at Longacres, looking out to Mount Rainier.

I could do that if only Longacres existed.

In 1989, the owners of Longacres, the Alhadeff family, sold the track to Boeing. A few years later, Boeing destroyed the track, and put up some office buildings.

From the air, when one flies into Seattle on certain approach routes, the racecourse is still visible even after all these years. The tall poplar trees are still growing.

And Mount Rainier is still there.

It makes you believe in God.

Particularly on those days when your belief in man is challenged.

Footnote: On a July 2007 visit to Seattle, I went out to Emerald Downs, the track that was built in Auburn, Washington, years after the death of Longacres. I was asked to give some commentary in the prerace show at the track (with an old Longacres PR guy, Joe Witthe). I gave out the eventual winner of the race.

He won.

Then he lost.

The stewards ruled my horse had interfered with the second-place runner, who was moved to first.

The owner of the official winner was the Alhadeff family.

Here is one relevant fact about horse racing.

Secretariat finished in the money in all but one of his twenty-one career starts. He was a fourth-place horse in his debut race.

Longacres

Horse Racing: We're Rich

Iwas at Five Mile Lake Park, doing another series of sprints, even though I wasn't all that fast. Maybe that's why I was doing so many sprints. It was the summer of 1981. I had one more season of tackle football to play at UNLV. As I finished up I saw some old friends from high school across the park. Chuck Mingori, Nick Metcalf, and George Laney were in a pickup basketball game. I joined them for a while, then pointed out how if we got in Chuck's car right then we could make it to Longacres in time for the final few races.

None of us had much money with us (or anywhere, for that matter), and it seemed like a very impetuous thing to do, so naturally, we got in Chuck's car and drove to Longacres.

I won some money on the ninth of ten races on the card and was sky high to reinvest. I threw out the idea that we each put in about thirty dollars and combine forces to try to win the final race five-dollar exacta. Back in those days at Longacres (and most tracks) there weren't many "exotic" wagering options as there are today. At Longacres, there was a first and second race daily double for two dollars and a tenth-race five-dollar exacta bet.

With the minutes to post winding down, each of us had submitted his top nominations for the race. We were going to add up the votes, find a consensus, and box as many horses as possible. (With $120 we could afford two "four horse boxes." If any two of the four horses in either box finished first and second we would hit the exacta.)

With about two minutes to post, Chuck Mingori announced he was backing out of the coalition. There wasn't time to talk him back into the project. The three of us remaining had ninety dollars to invest. We could box four horses at sixty and three more at thirty, for a total play of ninety dollars.

I don't remember what happened next. All I know is I went to the window as the horses were loading in the gate and read the teller the numbers just above my thumb, which was pinned down on my Longacres program.

It turns out that *under my thumb* were the numbers I was supposed to have played, the consensus of the picks from George, Nick, and me. What I had done instead was read Chuck's original numbers, a four-horse, five-dollar exacta box, totaling sixty dollars.

Who knows what I did with the other thirty dollars. Who cares?

As the horses broke from the gate, the four of us became separated. I ran upstairs to get the best view of the race from the grandstand. The others headed down to the far turn to watch the race from the rail.

As the animals turned for home I'd completely forgotten the names of the horses I'd backed (even Secretariat got reduced to "the 3 horse" when you come right down to it). But I did commit the numbers of our horses to short-term memory. And our numbers were running first through fourth as the field entered the stretch.

I don't remember how they all finished. What I do remember is that two of them finished one-two for the exacta. A very large exacta.

My three buddies were dragging themselves back to the grandstand. They looked like losers. And they were except for George and Nick. I punched George in the chest in celebration and started screaming, "We won! We won!" They were disbelieving. Most likely because rank outsiders had finished first and second. No one would bet on them. No one except someone who had done so by accident.

Chuck Mingori was and is a good guy. But that day he was bitter. He had a certain look in his eye. It said, "I am twenty-two years old.

I make $7 an hour and I just blew a chance at earning $1,235 in one minute thirty-eight seconds."

We filled Chuck's car with gas. We gave him a hundred dollars for having come up with the right numbers.

We didn't really notice Mount Rainier that day.

> Here is one more relevant fact about horse racing.
>
> The longest shot to win a Triple Crown Series race is Donerail, who hit the line first in the 1913 Kentucky Derby at 91–1. When he did so, it wasn't really a Triple Crown Series race, as the notion of the Triple Crown hadn't been considered yet. Still, he was 91–1.

Horse Racing:
The Dude Is Rich

Even adjusted for inflation, the score noted in the last chapter is child's play compared with what was taken down on Breeders' Cup day 2000. Peter Rotondo, a friend and a television executive for the National Thoroughbred Racing Association, left Churchill Downs with thirty thousand dollars cash.

But let's talk about the big winner.

The Dude. That's all I know him by. And the name is fitting.

The Dude is from England or maybe Ireland or maybe neither. But he rolled into Churchill on Breeders' Cup day with a bunch of fellas from overseas and a bunch of money, but nowhere near as much as he left with.

The official Breeders' Cup card hadn't started. There were a few warm-up races before the marquee action began.

The Dude ran into Peter with about two minutes to post before the second race on the card. The Dude knew very little about horse racing other than that players are to give a guy at the window money and then potentially receive more money from the teller when the horses have done their thing.

This economic model worked to perfection.

The Dude asked Peter who he liked in the race. Peter gave him a horse he loved as the "key horse" and listed about half a dozen others to put underneath on exactas and trifectas.

The Dude didn't listen to all the instructions and simply boxed

My favorite turf course: the downhill run at Santa Anita.

the first three horses Peter listed. *A three-horse one-hundred-dollar trifecta box.*

The Dude knew so little about horse racing, he didn't realize until he was told not to throw away his ticket that when the three horses ran in a one-two-three order other than the way his ticket listed the numbers, he was still a winner.

A big one.

The trifecta returned $5,370. *Fifty times.* Check my math, but I believe that's about $268,500.

Peter rolled out of the joint with thirty-thousand dollars as a reward.

Dude.

Here is still one more relevant fact about horse racing.

The longest shot to win a Breeders' Cup race is Arcangues, who won the Breeders' Cup Classic at 133–1.

Many people spell Breeder's Cup with the apostrophe in the wrong place. Breeders' Cup should be like that, to denote Breeders-possessive.

Hunting

In hunting, men get out of pickup trucks and kill deer.

The good guys who do this follow all the safety rules and use just about every part of the deer for food or clothing. The bad guys who do this don't follow the safety rules as well and are nearly as bad on the bad people scale as *the bad people of Starbucks who keep overcharging me for my triple tall Americanos.*

First of all, why does Starbucks use three different languages to describe the size of the drink cups? "Tall" sounds fairly English. "Grande" might be Spanish. And "venti"? Italian, I would guess.

Just go in and say "Medium."

I'm one of the many millions who has been seduced by the allure of hipness and coffee sold at a profit margin that could erase the federal deficit if the government had thought of this racket first. I like the music sold there. I like the general feel of the place. All seventy-six thousand Starbucks places. I'm not fooled by those hotels who proclaim, "We proudly serve Starbucks coffee." It has to be the real thing.

But the real thing keeps really screwing me.

My drink of choice is a so-called triple *tall* Americano. That's three shots of espresso and a little water. It tastes like a cup of black coffee, but stronger. I order the same thing nearly every time. I even go along with the fraudulent naming of a small cup as being a "tall" cup. Truth is, they also have a really small cup, what used to be called a "short" cup, but rumor has it they stopped promoting the fact that they carry "short" cups in deference to people who are not very tall.

Short people could be equally offended over the fact that Starbucks rubs it in by glorifying tall people with the selling of a small cup labeled a tall one.

For further background, a standard "tall" Americano comes with two shots of espresso and hot water filled to the brim of the cup (unless a customer asks for less water). A "grande" Americano comes with three shots of espresso and hot water, and a "venti" Americano comes with four shots of espresso and hot water.

My order is: "Triple tall Americano, very light on the water, about an inch, stop the whole process about halfway up the cup, please."

You've already figured out that I'm constantly ordering the ingredients of the grande Americano (three shots) but I want it delivered in a tall cup (less volume equates to a stronger drink) with very little water (an even stronger drink). In short, no offense, I want a strong-ass cup of coffee in their small cup.

Once I make the order, the person at the register then repeats it to the person manning (or womanning) the espresso station. That person is about the same distance from me as he or she is from the cashier and probably heard my order clearly. But it is customary and part of the drill for the cashier to repeat what I just said to the person who has just heard it from me. Starbucks promotes itself as a very green company, very hip to environmental issues. In fact, the drink cups are, I believe, made of deer hooves harvested by the good-guy hunters mentioned above. But for being so green, Starbucks has me and its cashiers depleting more fresh air than need be. Who knows how much energy had to be exerted by trees for having to work even harder than usual in their amazing photosynthesis process because of a ridiculous method used to place orders?

Once I've told the espresso maker what I want and once the cashier has also done that, the real drama begins. I glance at the cash register to see if, by some miracle, the cashier has priced my drink correctly.

The odds are 100 to 1.

For the record, I have ordered, in effect, a grande Americano.

A grande Americano costs $2.35 at most Starbucks. That price is about a 1,000 percent markup considering the true price of beans needed to make three espresso shots. But it was my choice to walk in the door. The base price is ridiculous but no one has a gun to my head to enter the facility. What's maddening is getting screwed involuntarily.

It's up to the cashier now. She hits the button for a "tall" Americano. That's $2.05. Then she hits the button for an "extra shot." Another 50 cents has been added. Once again, Starbucks is charging me in excess of the price of a grande Americano even though, once again, I have ordered the exact ingredients of a grande Americano.

Once again, an American worker has shown no ability to deviate.

Most of the time, I just pay the incorrect price but withhold any tip. I know it's coming in the same way I know a steak in New York City probably isn't really worth forty-nine dollars. But at least in New York City it says forty-nine dollars on the menu and at least in New York City the waiter doesn't charge me extra if I ask that the steak be placed on a plate slightly smaller than the one normally used.

My sister Nancy goes crazy when I begin my Starbucks debate. She says, "With all the money you make, why are you arguing over fifty cents?"

I say the same thing every time in reply. "Nancy, if you went to QFC and they had advertised hams were on special, two for the price of one, but when you got to the checkout they tried to charge you for two hams, would you say something, or just pay for both and say, 'What's another $11.95?' " Nancy always says, "That's different." I then tell her the amount of money one is being cheated out of is immaterial. It's the principle of the matter that counts. I waste money all the time on all sorts of things, like $49 steaks in New York City (where I never ask for a smaller plate). The point is, Starbucks already has high prices. The cashiers shouldn't be adding to the bill just because they cannot discern the fact that I've ordered the ingredients of one drink to be placed in a smaller contraption.

Me: I think you've overcharged me a bit.

Cashier: You had a triple tall Americano. That's a tall plus one shot.

Me: How many shots come in a grande Americano?

Cashier: Three.

Me: How many shots did I order?

Cashier: Three.

Me: Precisely. I asked for three shots, same as in a grande. It's just that I want them in a smaller cup, a tall cup as you call it here, so that the drink will be even stronger than usual.

Cashier: Why didn't you just ask for a grande with lots of room?

Me: Because I didn't want to have to carry around a cup the size of the kind they hand out at movie theaters. And by the way, lady, I have big hands.

Cashier: That's great. Look. I'm just entering into the system what you ordered. A tall with an extra shot.

Me: What does it matter what cup it's in? I'm saving you paper and water and you're trying to charge me extra money.

Cashier: Huh?

Me: What would you charge me if I asked that you take the three shots and pour them on the floor? Down the sink? On top of Old Smoky? A pound of hamburger is a pound of hamburger whether it's in cellophane or aluminum foil or fed to wild dogs. I asked for three shots, and a grande, as you've stipulated, comes with three shots. Why not charge me the price of the drink that comes with three shots, but don't charge me extra just because I want to save you hot water? I want a small, I mean tall, cup. Three shots.

Cashier: Huh?

Me: Did you see Jack Nicholson in *Five Easy Pieces* when the waitress said she couldn't deviate from the menu board? This is sort of like that but unlike Jack I'm not going to knock everything all over the floor. I'm just asking for three shots.

You have a drink that contains three shots. Why are you charging me extra for those three shots just because I want them in a smaller cup? And very little water.

Cashier: Did you want room for milk?

Me: Huh?

Cashier: You asked for extra room.

Me: No. I just want the room. The extra room is for air.

Cashier: Huh?

Me: If you put three shots in a cup that is smaller than the cup that normally takes three shots *and* then you don't fill the smaller cup up very much with hot water, it will be a stronger drink. I want a strong cup of coffee in a small cup.

Cashier: I thought you wanted a triple tall Americano.

It goes on this way for several uncomfortable minutes. My sister Nancy usually kills herself, then comes back to life to say, "Was it really worth all that?"

Then I say to everyone: *"YOU CANNOT BE SERIOUS!"*

At this point the manager comes over and presses some buttons, and I get what I should have gotten in the first place: three shots in a tall cup, not a lot of water, and at the same price the three shots would have cost had they been poured into a cup Starbucks calls grande.

I usually say some nice things to soften the mood and then end up tipping the baristas the change. In the end, though they all think I'm a jerk, the arguments I made were on their behalf. More change is left over to go into the tip bin.

On the way out of Starbucks, as I begin to enjoy my strong-ass cup of coffee, I realize that the warning on the side of the cup about the coffee temperature is accurate: I've just burned my face beyond recognition. My sister Nancy cannot recognize the person who is taking the lid off his cup of coffee to inspect just how high the water was poured. The water was filled to the brim. The person who made the triple tall Americano did not listen to the repeated requests for "light water" or to "stop when the cup is about half full."

I walk back to the counter. I cannot look the cashier or the manager in the eye. It is too painful at this point.

I walk past the counter, directly to the barista.

Me: I'm sorry. After all that I have to ask you to try again.
Barista: What's the problem?
Me: The problem is I asked for very light water on my triple tall
   Americano.

Barista: Did you want room for cream?

Me: No. I wanted room for room. (I show the barista my drink.) The water is about one-sixteenth of an inch below the brim.

Barista: Huh?

Me: Let me put it to you this way: I asked for light water and you filled it to the top. If I hadn't said anything about a lesser amount of water would you have just kept pouring water into the cup, right over the sides of the cup? Would you have just flooded the Central Connecticut Valley with water? I mean, I asked for light water and this is what you did. How much water would have been put in had I not brought up the amount of water?

At this point, Nancy kills herself again.

Barista: Huh?

Good hunters make their own coffee and brew it over an open flame. They then put out the fire and bury the ashes with dirt so as to prevent forest fires.

Here is a relevant fact about hunting.

A 2006 study by the Outdoor Industry Foundation suggests that nearly 12 percent of Americans sixteen years and older (26.4 million people) said they hunted with a gun or bow in the previous year.

Jai Alai

"Jai alai" is pronounced "hi-a-lie." But there's a lot more to the game than that. For starters, you have to fly to Florida to see it played. That's unless you live in Florida. It's also unless you are at an offtrack betting facility, in which case you can see the game played on a ten-inch monitor at your little gaming table while you're waiting for a horse race to run. Or, if you came to the offtrack betting facility only to watch hi-a-lie, you could be sitting there wondering why the name of the place isn't "Off-Hi-a-lie Betting Facility." If that's happening right now, why did you bring a book to the Off-Hi-a-lie Betting Facility? You should be looking through a program that details how Ortega has been doing in his last ten games and how Laca has done when paired with Trueba.

I don't know if Laca and Trueba still play hi-a-lie. But I do know they played a mean game back in the late seventies, early eighties. Those were the days, hi-a-lie's greatest days in America. Maybe the game thrived to an even greater degree before that time but I'm not going to get out of Microsoft Word to look it up. Not at this hour.

I was introduced to the sport in 1979, my first spring at UNLV. The game was played at the fronton located at the far end of the old MGM Hotel. Hartford and Milford, Connecticut, had frontons then. So did Newport, Rhode Island. Florida had and still has some frontons and now is the only state where the sport survives.

If we all band together, we could bring the sport back to its former prominence. Or we could just keep doing whatever it was we were doing before this sentence was read.

If you think you've never seen jai alai, try to recall the last time you saw the old TV show *Miami Vice*. In the opening credits, jai alai is pictured. When you watch *Miami Vice* the next time, take a poll in your living room. Who is cooler: Don Johnson or David Caruso? Caruso is on *CSI: Miami* and that show doesn't even have jai alai pictured in its opening credits. Plus, no one but David Caruso talks that way.

Jai alai is similar to racquetball in that there is a server, there is an over-under service receive line, the ball cannot bounce twice, and it hurts like hell to get struck in the face with it. You would have to go to the doctor, it hurts so much to be struck in the face with a jai alai ball.

Doctor: What happened?
You: I got hit in the face with a jai alai ball.
Doctor: That ball is more accurately called a "pelota."
You: I didn't know that.
Doctor: Who is cooler: Don Johnson or David Caruso?

Even if you hadn't been hit in the face with a jai alai ball, I'd have informed you that it is really called a pelota. I don't know if jai alai experts call a baseball a pelota or if they just call it a baseball. The wicker-basket-looking thing that pelotas are launched with is called a cesta.

That's about all you need to know about jai alai except that unlike racquetball, there are three walls instead of four.

The other thing you need to know about jai alai is that a lot of people believe it is fixed. But who cares about those people? Money is still paid to those with winning tickets after a game of jai alai has been played. To those who question the integrity of the game because in one instance they see a player climbing one of the three walls to make an incredibly gifted catch and in one motion fling an unreturnable shot, and then the next instance they see the same player drop a pelota that was more or less delivered to him with room service, I say: I've seen Jerry Rice drop an easy pass.

But the other thing to know about jai alai, besides the fact that Jerry Rice dropped a pass once, is that in the late seventies and early eighties in Las Vegas, Nevada, my friends and I *controlled the game.* My memory could be off a bit on this point or it could be we were delusional at the time. Also, we had about forty dollars in capital between us. But money does not always equal power. Just ask Bill Gates. He would probably give away the rest of his money if he could control one point in a game of jai alai. Look how much he's given away already and that's without having had any impact on jai alai.

As in racquetball, the server serves to begin the game. He must place the pelota somewhere between the over-under lines. This is why, when a jai alai player we were rooting against was just about to release the pelota from his cesta we would scream, as loud as possible, *"Under!"* Sometimes, just to keep things fresh, we would scream, *"Over!"*

"Under!" was just plain funnier.

Given that some people had said the games were fixed, we sort of feared that we might end up out in the desert because of our yelling *"Under!"* Succeeding in making the server serve under the under line could have thrown out of sync whatever it was that was being fixed, and I'm not one who thinks they were all fixed, given the fact that Jerry Rice dropped a ball once. There were about seventy-five fans watching the games at the Las Vegas fronton. That is to say, we made up about 15 percent of the total live audience.

It was me, Robin McClarren, Thumper White, Ray Crouse, Jimmy Sandusky, and Keith Reardon. Keith and I held our own games of jai alai in our apartment hallway with a taped-up roll of toilet paper.

These were jai alai's greatest days.

Not enough people came to the fronton in Las Vegas to yell *"Under!"* or *"Over!"* or even to just sit there and let the game go on without trying to impose any influence on it. One day, I don't recall which day, they closed the fronton for good. They not only closed the fronton at the MGM, they moved the hotel. The old fronton is now a part of the newer Bally's Casino. Except it's no longer a part. It was remodeled.

It is now a parking lot.

Under.

> *Here is an interesting fact about jai alai.*
>
> *It is so interesting it is italicized. It is italicized because I cannot figure out how to get the italics function to stop. Anyway, it's a hell of a fact and here it is: The ball used in jai alai, a pelota, often reaches speeds of up to 150 mph. The fastest speed clocked was 188 mph.*

Modern Indoor Tackle Football

To appreciate modern indoor tackle football fully, one must first be educated in olden-time indoor tackle football.

Our home growing up had a large rectangular living room. This isn't to say it was a bad living room. On the contrary, it had a picture window with a view of the lake we lived on, Star Lake, and was picture perfect for indoor tackle football.

We would first get a ride from my sister Nancy to 7-Eleven for the purchase of several ninety-nine-cent pizzas, a few megasized bottles of pop, and maybe some Red Vines. It was going to be a party. There was Danny Sargent; the Dorans, Shawn and Dennis; Mark Sansaver; and me.

The game was tournament style, one on one. The quarterback started about ten feet in from the picture window facing the front door. Back in those days, we never locked the front door, even while away on vacation. This was partly because those were different times (the late sixties and seventies) and partly because we *didn't have a key to our home.* I don't know if my dad lost the key or if the house just didn't come with one. No one ever broke in. But then, no one had to break in. They could just walk in.

Therefore, I have no idea if anyone ever came in and took anything. If somebody did, I don't miss whatever was taken.

So the quarterback faced the front door, while the defender faced the quarterback, his hands reaching back to touch the door, his starting point. At the snap of the ball (actually a slap of the ball) the quarterback had three seconds (counted by one of the players not in the game) to release the ball or face a loss of down. Each chair, couch, table, stereo console, had a different value for yardage gained based on the difficulty level of throwing a pass to that "receiver" and making the ball land there.

The rocking chair my grandma Alma sat in all the time (though not during these games) was good for only five yards. You had to complete two passes to Grandma's chair to get a first down. That very chair is the one my grandma used to accidentally kill three baby chicks in the late 1960s. My sister Carolee had received the chicks as gifts from a kid named Rocky Robinson, whose family, I guess, had a surplus of baby chicks. Carolee had wrapped them in a blanket and left them on the rocking chair while she ran to her room for something. Moments later, Grandma sat down to watch her "stories" (*As the World Turns* was her favorite). Carolee came back into the living room and asked what Grandma had done with her babies.

It turns out Grandma had killed them.

That night my mom made chicken for dinner.

The ball we used was a pillow football in Washington State University colors. It was soft to the touch but just firm enough that if the ball was thrown a bit too hard it could bounce off the intended target and be intercepted if the defender got into the right position. Once the ball had made contact with the "receiver," the defender could not touch it, lest he be called for interference. He could make an interception if the ball rolled out of the receiver's imaginary window of opportunity and began a free fall toward the carpet.

The ten-yard reception was the stereo console (we played 45s and 33s back then) on the far right side of the field. A twenty-yard reception was my dad's favorite chair in the left corner, and an automatic touchdown came by throwing successfully to the wicker chair that we'd import from the dining room.

The games were lively. We'd play a pair of ten-minute (clock running) halves. There were plenty of arguments, plenty of bad ninety-nine-cent 7-Eleven pizzas.

7-Eleven is worthy of its own chapter. Imagine a store that stayed open all the way until 11 p.m.

Modern indoor tackle football is an entirely new game, a developmental league intended to pass along the great game of indoor tackle football to a new generation. Right now, it has at least three players.

There's my daughter Riley (eight years old at this writing), my daughter Annie (six), and me.

The field is small, much smaller than the one used in olden-day indoor tackle football. The goal line is the leather couch that no one ever sits on. All four of us in my family (including my wife, Laura) pile onto a much smaller couch whenever we convene to watch television or a DVD. Our house is twice the size of the house I grew up in, five times larger than what we need, yet the four of us squeeze together and use an area no more than fifteen square feet. We are a close family.

The kids aren't supposed to climb on the furniture. I've heard myself actually say to them, "No climbing on the furniture!" I don't know why I say this. I could care less if they climb on the furniture. I would if I were them. It's fun to climb on the furniture. It's even more fun to climb on it, then jump off. I think I say "No climbing on the furniture!" because it makes me feel like an adult. Screw that. I'm going to climb on the furniture with them tomorrow. What a stupid rule. If I let them dive for touchdown passes onto the leather couch that no one ever sits on, why do I care if they climb on it? I don't. From now on they can climb on the leather couch. They can eat on the leather couch. They can use ink pens on it. Ink pens with sparkle-fleck princess ink. Permanent, nonwashable sparkle-fleck princess ink. Who cares? At least that stupid leather couch will get some use that way.

The main use for the leather couch that no one sits on is to stand as a symbol of excellence for the girls in modern indoor tackle football. Each child knows ten individual pass routes, their favorite being the "5-route," a post route that has them ending up in the middle cushion of the leather couch no one ever sits on. They run about ten feet, angle at forty-five degrees toward the middle of the couch, and look for the ball, a soft Green Bay Packers glow-in-the-dark model. Riley once made a historic Lynn Swann Super Bowl–like catch on a 5-route. She was horizontal to the ground, in full extension over the leather couch no one sits on, when she reached out and pulled in the Green Bay Packer glow-in-the-dark model football.

I have never been more proud of her.

Annie runs better routes, if truth be told. But as long as we're involved in all this truth telling here, she has caught exactly three passes in her two-year career. They hit her in the hands, they hit her in the chest, they hit her on the side of the face. She doesn't care. In fact, she likes it when I pretend to be a mean coach and yell at her for not catching the ball. She would thrive under Bobby Knight. If only Bobby Knight coached modern indoor tackle football.

Sometimes we call plays from a huddle, sometimes from the line of scrimmage. The only problem with that is that both girls have learned the exact same offensive package. When one is playing defense she can simply listen to the number of the route that is called and cheat to the area designated in the play call. Riley and I have developed a secondary code to fool any defender who would squat in the "out route" area (over by the fireplace). I cannot give away the code, as Annie might be reading this. Then again, by the time this is printed, Annie will likely have learned her own coding. It's a difficult thing showing equal love to two children.

Annie likes to hold huddles. It's partly because we can do something in secret from her sister and partly because she likes me to make up silly trick plays. When she calls the plays in the huddle they often make no sense whatsoever. I just nod a lot (just like in meetings with my bosses) and wait for her to make a route cut before I throw the ball.

Just the other day my dream come true arrived in the mail. The local tackle football league sent out a notice so as to draw more support of the peewee divisions. The girls aren't eligible for tackle football just yet, but on the same form there was an e-mail address to contact the league regarding flag football. Both girls are eligible for that.

There was also a paragraph or two about cheerleading. Children can sign up to be cheerleaders. Cheerleading has nothing at all to do with modern indoor tackle football.

Just to be fair I told the girls they had some options. I told them, "You can sign up to play flag football with other children your age, which will be tons of fun. Or you can just be a cheerleader for the other kids who are really playing football, and this probably won't be so great and will take up way too much time. You won't get to ride your bikes because of all the time it will take to practice cheerleading. There's probably no chance you want to do this."

I had laid out the options fairly, not pushing the girls in any one direction.

When I told them about all this, they were just getting out of their bath one night. Their mother was about to ready them for a picture session with a local photographer. They knew they were going to be allowed to wear a teeny-tiny bit of makeup for the photography session.

They both chose cheerleading.

Here is a relevant fact about something.

The NFL's first playoff game was played indoors at Chicago Stadium in 1932 because of bitter cold and heavy snow. The Chicago Bears beat the Portsmouth (Ohio) Spartans 9–0 with Bronco Nagurski and Red Grange connecting on a two-yard touchdown pass. A two-yard pass would have been good for only a five-yard gain in our indoor tackle football league. Plus, Nagurski didn't have 7-Eleven pizza to nourish his body.

Second Time-out

One time at UNLV I was standing on the sideline (where I spent a lot of time as a second-string quarterback). But this time, I was on the sideline because I was in the game. A time-out had been called. I went over the play call with my coach, Tony Knapp, in a very short amount of time. There was nothing left to say, but I lingered on the sidelines with Coach Knapp and the assistants. Finally Coach Knapp said, "Well, what are you doing? Go out there and run the play!"

I told him, "I'm just staying over here for a little longer so the other side thinks we know what we are doing."

Orienteering

The only reason I have ever heard of orienteering is because somebody from *Scholastic Sports America*, the old TV show ESPN ran (Chris Fowler, your host) in the late eighties and early nineties, called me and said I'd be paid as much as $250 to go do a TV story on orienteering. The year was 1987. I had no idea why anyone from *Scholastic Sports America* would be calling me. It couldn't have been because I was any good on TV. I'd been on the air for all of about six months. Likely, it was due to the fact that the orienteering event was taking place near Tacoma, Washington, nearer my TV station than those twenty-five miles away in Seattle.

I didn't really have anything to wear. What do you wear to orienteering anyway?

I ended up in a ski coat. I looked like a dorkmaster and wandered around in the woods trying to figure out why the youngsters were running by me in what looked like part cross-country run, part treasure hunt. There wasn't all that much to figure out because that's pretty much what they were doing. As near as I could tell competitors in orienteering are told to run into the woods and look for some kind of signs. As much as I can recall the signs they were looking for were signs.

The signs told them where to run next, which in all but the last case was to another sign. I assume the final sign read: "Run to the finish line." I really don't know, because I left before it was over.

It was cold and raining. I had a crappy ski coat.

I told you it was a ski coat and not a rain coat, right?

Now that I think about it, I believe the runners also carried a map. Maybe that's why I wrote the thing about the treasure hunt.

I don't remember much at all. In fact, there's some chance I didn't even get $250. Maybe it was more like $100. But that was okay. I was already working for KSTW-TV and was able to run the same terrible story I gave to ESPN on my own station. Or maybe I wasn't. Maybe I sent all the tapes to *Scholastic Sports America* and wasn't allowed to run any of the material on my show. Why would *Scholastic Sports America* give up the rights to such a fine piece of telejournalism as has been described here?

I do recall orienteering as being very memorable.

The most memorable part of this chapter for you may be that section that was highlighted in bold.

It just turned bold one day when I was writing this stupid book. I tried to make it not bold. I pushed every button on my computer. In doing so, I wound up buying a bunch of stuff I didn't want over the Internet. I can't figure out how to make them take it back, whoever they are. I wish I'd bought that crap from Nordstrom. They'll take anything back. I love sports.

Here is another relevant thing.

The four types of orienteering recognized by the International Orienteering Federation are foot orienteering, mountain bike orienteering, ski orienteering, and trail orienteering. So, you're telling me I could have done four ESPN *Scholastic Sports America* stories?

Ping-Pong

Ping-Pong is sometimes called table tennis. Probably so that it sounds like something more closely related to a mainstream sport.

It's a big deal in China. We know that because Chinese people never win at Wimbledon. Right now, if Chinese people didn't like the way this story was going, they could cash in all the U.S. Treasury bonds they own and our economy would collapse. That would really suck.

As for Ping-Pong, the game is played with one or two players on each side. When two players are on a side, one or two of them always get hit with a paddle, usually in the arm, but sometimes across the face. This slows the game down. If it happens to you, grab a bag of ice and apply it to your arm or face. In cartoons they always use steak to bring down the swelling. If the Chinese sell all those bonds you should use ice, which is more or less free, because at that point steak will cost too much.

This is almost getting into the neighborhood of one of those Ben Stein books on economics. I've never seen him play Ping-Pong. Or table tennis.

Good Ping-Pong players, like the Chinese, play about twenty to thirty feet removed from the table, and this makes the game seem a lot more like tennis whether the Chinese cash in all their bonds or not.

Additionally, people there actually pay money (I think the Chinese monetary unit is a title to an American home, but I could be wrong) to watch Ping-Pong, and they cheer loudly when there is a long rally, when someone makes a spectacular save, or when someone sells a U.S. Treasury bond.

In American Ping-Pong, the only people watching are those who are waiting for the godforsaken game taking place to end (usually at 11 or 21 points). The people watching are usually in somebody's rec room, basement, or garage. This explains the poor attendance figures in American Ping-Pong.

You should always have more than one Ping-Pong ball when staging a game. This way, you don't have to quit when one of the dorkier people in your playing group steps on a loose Ping-Pong ball and crushes it, rendering it useless.

Ping-Pong is a safer game than dodgeball (see "Dodgeball") for underdeveloped seventh graders, but it is oftentimes just as humiliating. This is especially true if a Chinese student is staying at an underdeveloped seventh grader's house in some sort of cultural exchange program. The worst thing would be for the underdeveloped seventh grader to have his ass kicked in Ping-Pong by the visiting Chinese student while the visiting Chinese student's parents sell a bunch of U.S. Treasury bonds, if Chinese people and not just the Chinese government are allowed to own them.

After being destroyed by the Chinese student, the underdeveloped seventh grader should come back with: "That's great, Ping. Let's see you win Wimbledon with that little wooden paddle."

If the Chinese kid comes back with "You cannot be serious!" then he wins the argument.

In conclusion, Chinese people are awesome at table tennis. Please don't sell off all the U.S. Treasury bonds at the same time. That would suck. You win. You're better than us at table tennis and Ping-Pong and have a lot of our bonds. We challenge you to orienteering.

Here is another relevant thing that is actually pretty relevant compared with some of the others.

In 1973, the *Guinness Book of World Records* documented the most hits in a sixty-second table tennis rally — 173 by Jackie Bellinger and Lisa Lomas of Great Britain.

Rock Throwing

I really don't know what the statute of limitations is for throwing rocks at cars and trains. I have high hopes it is something short of thirty-six years. If not, what could the penalty be for taking out the driver's-side window of a 1972 Ford?

Besides, I was just an accomplice in that. I threw short, on purpose.

The year was 1972, as you figured out from the thirty-six-years thing (and the Ford thing). My friend Mark Sansaver and I were on a road trip with our tackle football team to Oregon. The two of us were staying with a kid on the team we played that week.

He had a nice family who lived on a big farm right across the street from some railroad tracks. Mark and I drove a motor vehicle for the first time that week. The kid's parents had no problem with the three of us bombing around in the family pickup truck.

Then it got dangerous.

It was just before three o'clock. Mark and I were informed that a train would be coming soon. Time to park the truck, walk across the street, pick up rocks, and blast the hell out of whatever came by on the train.

This time, brand-new automobiles, being transported to car dealerships.

Mark and I looked at each other for guidance. Neither of us knew what the other would do, rock in hand. I had heard "When in Rome . . . throw rocks at trains with kids who are allowed to drive pickup trucks at 50 mph on their parents' farm."

It wasn't enough for this kid to have stripped the gears on his father's old truck. Now he was out to do damage on new models.

I heard the first glass break and thought to myself, "The kid has a good arm."

Mark and I didn't say anything to each other but we both came to the same conclusion. On that day we were just fine with being judged to have weak arms. We both threw short, missing the cars on purpose, missing our chance to break the left-side windows of Ford Pintos.

In the game that Saturday, we threw long. We trashed the Oregon kids. Mark's father, the late Bill Sansaver, was never more proud. Not because Mark and I showed a little maturity and didn't vandalize automobiles, but because we showed maturity in the game. The Oregon kids had coaches in the huddle the entire way, calling plays, coaching up the kids on this or that. Bill Sansaver had taught us what's what during the week leading to the game. He let me call all the plays. He told me it was the best thing he'd ever been involved in on a football field. Not being involved, that is. He was proud that he'd already imparted what it was he wanted executed.

Bill would have been proud also of the decision making Mark and I made the following spring when the two of us went on another sports exchange, this time to Victoria, British Columbia.

This time, instead of attacking trains, our host and a teammate of his took us out on the town to *throw rocks at houses.*

The Canadian kids had a plan. We would hop two buses and get several neighborhoods away from where they lived. We were led down a dark street. Then the Canadians started firing away at a couple of houses that stood in a neighborhood below the hill we were on. They began throwing (and breaking windows) before Mark and I knew what was going on. We knew enough not to throw. We also knew to run.

Not much was spoken on the bus rides home though we should have told the Canadians how much they'd like Oregon.

This is another sports fact.

According to research conducted by the World Rock Paper Scissors Society, men tend to start with "rock" and women with "scissors" when playing rock, paper, scissors, which I call scissors, paper, rock, but the society didn't research what some men call the game.

Rowing

In rowing, a bunch of men or women sit in a boat and row as hard as they can while another person, the coxswain, yells at them to row even harder.

Wikipedia says that "coxswain" means "boat servant." If it's in Wikipedia, it must be true.

But how can the person who yells at the others who are rowing as hard as they can to row even harder be considered a servant? If he's a servant, what method would one who is referred to as "boss man" use to make people who are rowing as hard as they can row harder?

I figure the people who grow up to be coxswains are the same ones who sat around cracking up for hours about the fact that in badminton the thing people hit back and forth is called a shuttlecock (see "Badminton").

Anyway, in the United States, in rowing, a bunch of people get in a boat and get yelled at to row harder.

In another boat, or in several other boats, the same thing is going on. Usually these people who are either rowing as hard as they can or being yelled at to row even harder than they can all go to college. They row as hard as they can or yell at others to row even harder than they can before an audience of parents, mostly.

Sometimes newspaper people, who adore the tradition of rowing as hard as possible while being yelled at to row even harder, will show up and then write stories about the spectacle and then put the stories in an actual newspaper.

For some reason it's a real big deal at prestigious colleges such as Harvard. Most of the kids who go to Harvard are really smart and will end up owning boats driven by other people, though no oars will be involved and there won't be that much yelling. You'd think, being so smart, all the people at Harvard who want to be on the rowing team would try out for the part where you get to yell at people to row harder than they already can. It's management training.

The drivers of the boats owned by those who went to Harvard will not be called coxswains even though they are servants. They will be called boat drivers.

The sport is particularly popular in England and other countries like that. It's considered a big deal when our best college boat people and those who yell at our best college boat people beat the best boat people and those who yell at boat people from England and countries like that. When that happens the newspaper people who showed up with the parents at the U.S. boat races get to write longer stories and maybe include a color photograph.

Those who are on rowing teams wake up very early in the morning to practice rowing while being yelled at or to practice yelling at people rowing a boat. This is great preparation for waking up very early in the morning to go to a job and either be yelled at or yell at people.

Education is very important.

> This thing is becoming encyclopedic. Here's yet another sports fact. Rowing is the oldest college sport in America.

Skateboarding

Skateboarding used to be the sport that kids wearing flannel shirts who were stoned out of their minds did on sidewalks while mowing over grandmothers and not saying, "Excuse me, ma'am."

Now, some of what's above is true but they do it on TV and get paid money.

I don't know if Tony Hawk was or is stoned out of his mind but he made skateboarding (and eventually, many other nontraditional sports) acceptable and profitable and helped keep grandmothers safe on sidewalks.

They can now do stuff with skateboards that only gymnasts with springboards were doing twenty years ago. Or maybe they were doing these kind of things with skateboards twenty years ago but we didn't know it because they weren't on TV.

Then somebody (ESPN) figured out you could leave the skateboarders in their flannel shirts, but take them off the sidewalks and stick them inside TV sets. Then everybody, but mostly ESPN, would make a bunch of money.

The skateboarders then figured out they didn't need the flannel shirts as much as they needed shirts that had names of companies on them. Those companies would then give them a bunch of money to do stuff that twenty years ago only gymnasts could do and only with springboards.

It wasn't exactly the Olympics but the Extreme Games (later changed to X-Games, later changed to Summer X and Winter X but not Spring or Fall X) were born. Skateboarding was just one of many underpublicized games that made it inside the TV set. They also had a sport where two people would jump out of an airplane, one of whom had a camera on his head like Albert Brooks in *Real People*, a good movie. The guy with the camera would aim his head (and thus, camera) at the guy without the camera. The guy without the camera would do all sorts of flips and twists and crazy stuff. Eventually, both jumpers would pull their cords and a parachute would open. Skateboarders would look up to the sky and one of them would say, "Whoa, dude. Two guys just jumped out of that plane and one of them has a camera on his head."

Another skateboarder would say, "Dude. That's nothing. Tony Hawk is a millionaire."

Here is a fact.

During the 1999 X-Games, Tony Hawk became the first skateboarder to pull off the "900" skateboarding trick, which requires two and a half turns in the air off a vert ramp, and which mocked all the other skateboarders who had planned on unveiling the "899."

Sliding

The only equipment necessary in sliding is a piece of torn-off cardboard, preferably from a large box that held a refrigerator.

Participants climb a small hill, often found behind a junior high or high school, often leading to the football field below.

The winner is the person who slides to the bottom of the hill on the torn-off cardboard first.

This is a stupid sport, yes. But the printed explanation here gives us all an emotional breather after having just dealt with the extreme nature of people jumping out of planes with cameras on their heads.

Sliding is a sometimes dangerous sport and participants should wear helmets even if their friends call them dorks for doing so. Absent a helmet, sliders run the risk of ending up with a concussion, the effects of which can show up at any time, including, for me, now.

I just had déjà vu again.

Again.

This stems from the time I was sliding behind Thomas Jefferson High School with Mark Sansaver and his brother Bruno.

I just had déjà vu again.

I'm also again seeing that my computer puts the little squiggly things over the word déjà even if I don't write the word vu.

Deja squiggly vu. It didn't do it that time. What is going on? That must have been some concussion.

Maybe it doesn't do it when déjà is capitalized. It just did it when it wasn't capitalized.

Let me try.

Déjà.

Wait. It did it. Do you think it didn't do it about five lines ago be-cause I wrote the word "squiggly" just after Deja? Wait. It didn't do it again. That must have been some concussion. I can barely work my way through this stupid chapter and the only thing it has to do with is buying a refrigerator and sliding down a hill with the Sansavers. You don't have to buy a refrigerator to play the sport. Just find some cardboard. Where was I? Helmets. Use a helmet. I wish I had that day I got the concussion. Then again, had I worn a helmet maybe I wouldn't have the cornerstone material for this great book.

We were sliding down the hill behind the high school. It wasn't really "our" high school at the time. We were in junior high. Also, I don't know why I used quote marks just a couple sentences back. I hate it when people overuse quote marks, especially in person. I know a guy who uses them so often he does so inappropriately. As in: I am going to "lunch," does anyone want to "go"?

The story just above is better told in person. Ask me to tell it if I see you.

Anyway, I think we can get through the rest of this without any more quote marks. Who knew about the squiggly lines when it comes to déjà vu? Now we know.

We were sliding down the hill, without helmets, and my card-board slide took off like a rocket ship. I fell backward, quickly, and hit my head on the ground with great force. We kept sliding for an-other hour or so even though I didn't know who or where I was.

The day I wrote this, I went to "lunch" at Santa Anita Race Park.

The cardboard was so slick and I was going so fast that I flew backward like I had taken off in a rocket ship.

I'm having "déjà vu" again.

I remember saying, "I hit my head, hard."

That's all I remember. I remember having déjà vu right when it happened. Now, when I have the déjà vu about the fact I hit my head, I'm not sure if I'm having déjà vu about that, which isn't really déjà vu, it's more of a recollection, or if I am having the déjà vu about whatever it was I had the déjà vu about when I hit my head.

It really "hurt."

Today I had "breakfast," and "lunch" and "dinner" but not all at once and not all at Santa Anita "Race Park."

I do know I hit my head hard that day at Thomas Jefferson on the hill leading to somebody's tackle football field.

There's no way that sliding will get approved in time to be an Olympic sport for the Games in China. If it actually were to happen, I'd probably question the whole thing and believe I was having "déjà vu."

Man, the people who bought this book are stupid.

They are probably having déjà vu about the last time they were so stupid.

"Again."

Here's something that may or may not be relevant.

It took former major leaguer Cecil Fielder a record 1,097 games played to steal his first base. He finished his career with two stolen bases.

Snowball Fighting

In snowball fighting teams are divided into equal numbers and everyone throws snowballs at each other until somebody gets hit in the face, cries, and goes home.

Then somebody's mom makes everyone hot chocolate.

A derivative of this game is snowball fighting at cars, which is dangerous and wrong and should not be done at any time. There is no question the kids I met from Oregon and Victoria, B.C., threw snowballs at cars.

The kid from Oregon already threw rocks at trains (see "Rock Throwing"), so he probably didn't have a lot of reservations about throwing snowballs at cars. In fact, throwing snowballs at cars after having thrown rocks at trains was something of a regression for him on the hooligan scale.

The kids from Victoria, B.C., already threw rocks at houses (again, see "Rock Throwing"), so for them to throw mere snowballs at cars would have had them losing all hooligan credibility. The only way they'd throw snowballs at cars was if the snowballs had rocks in them.

Our most celebrated snowball-throwing episode came on a December night in 1972, our seventh-grade year. We were hiding in the woods by the tennis courts at Glenn Nelson Park, taking turns blasting car after car that came by during a rare snowy winter in Seattle. Unlike some of the bullies you read about in the dodgeball chapter, we really did show some restraint and aimed for less dangerous parts of the cars, the side doors, back windows, and trunk.

There were five of us throwing that night: the Doran twins, Shawn and Dennis; Mark Sansaver; Dave LeClair; and me. All of us were successful hitting the target on one particular barrage of snowballs. The car's driver hit the brakes hard. We saw the red taillights through the snowfall. We froze in place when the car came to a stop. As the car took off once more we let our guard down. We started packing snow for the next assault. Suddenly we heard branches breaking, twigs snapping on the ground, feet running fast through the snow, approaching our staging area.

Instead of running we all tried to hide. Behind a tree, in the bushes, and in plain sight. One by one, our attacker rounded us up. He looked to be really old, about seventeen or eighteen. He was practically a man.

It was so dark I couldn't see who it was, but his voice sounded familiar. And it was. Scott Forbes, a senior at the high school, a friend of the family and the boyfriend of Darcy Berube, my sister Nancy's best friend.

For about thirty seconds he gave us a scared-straight speech about the dangers of throwing snowballs at cars. Then he reached down for something. It was snow. Scott Forbes packed himself a couple snowballs. He stayed in the woods with us for another hour. We blasted car after car together.

If there is any moral to this story it's probably that Scott Forbes had a great arm.

This is actually a pretty good fact. Way better than some of the other facts we tried to slip in to make this seem more like a sports book.

The throwing of snowballs actually helped ignite the Boston Massacre, which in turn would help spark the American Revolution.

Soccer

In soccer, six-year-old players chase the ball and run together as one big glob of humanity, don't understand spacing, pass the ball to a teammate exactly once during the course of an entire season, pull each other's pants down, kick each other in the shins, and cry after the game if the mom in charge of bringing orange wedges, snacks, and juice boxes doesn't bring any of that because her kid stayed home, having had his pants pulled down and his shins kicked in the last game, plus, by not going to soccer, he could instead go to some other six-year-old's birthday party and receive a companion gift.

Apparently that's not the same experience in other countries, which is why we don't win very often when matched against the greatest teams in the world in something called the World Cup.

I'm taking a break from soccer to have a snack and juice box.

Here is a somewhat relevant story about soccer.

Eric Benz was great at throwing the ball back in high school. One of the other stars of our high school team, Jim McKay, was able to grow facial hair in about third grade. By high school, he could grow a full beard in three days. For this, we called him Charles Manson. Sometimes we just called him Charley. I didn't play spring sports in high school because I sucked at baseball and was too slow for track and field. I instead worked for the sports section of the school paper and covered some baseball and soccer. Sometimes at the soccer games I would

act as the public address announcer. One time, after a spectacular bicycle kick, I uttered over the PA system, "Manson, with
the spectacular bicycle kick." Manson's parents didn't think
that calling their son Manson was as funny as the rest of us, or
as funny as Manson thought it was, and complained to the
school principal. I was told not to call him Manson anymore.
This seemed like a restriction on my freedom of speech in the
same way an ESPN boss told me to quit saying, "The players
are gay," whenever I saw baseball players jumping up and
down at home plate to celebrate a game-ending home run.

Six-year-old soccer players who chase the ball together and
run all over the field like one big glob of humanity, and don't
pass but once a season, pull each other's pants down, and kick
each other in the shins, but who *do* get boxed drinks, orange
wedges, and snacks when the other kid shows up and his mom
doesn't stay out at a tavern and forget to stop at the store on
the way to the game, are gay.

Tackle Football

Tackle football is the greatest sport in the world and everyone knows it.

Tackle football was invented in the 1800s, or a long time ago, by a man who thought it would be cool if one man with a ball struggled to move toward a white line painted on some grass while a bunch of men (Team B) tried to throw him to the ground. The man with the ball had a bunch of other men (Team A) trying to help him avoid being thrown to the ground by the bunch of men trying to throw him to the ground (Team B). The man with the ball would begin the play without the ball. Another man on his team (Team A) would bend over and pass the ball between his legs to the man who would eventually have the ball and try to avoid being thrown to the ground. The sight of a man passing the ball between his legs to a man who wanted to run the ball while avoiding being thrown to the ground made the men who wanted to throw the man with the ball to the ground (Team B) laugh hysterically. Later, when the method of starting a play was changed and a man without the ball *stuck his hands between the legs* of the man who had the ball and who was bending over, the players on Team B laughed even more hysterically.

This is why the running game in football got off to such a successful start.

When the men on the team that wanted to throw the man with the ball to the ground stopped laughing so much at the same joke, over and over, the running game didn't work as well.

At that point somebody on the team with the guy who didn't want

Brett Favre

to be thrown to the ground had somebody kick the ball between metal uprights and over a metal bar.

It *is* the greatest sport in the world and everyone knows it.

Everyone except the four billion or so people who believe soccer is the greatest game in the world. Most of them call soccer football. They call our football crap.

In America, there are eleven men on each side. Sometimes, in rare cases, some of the eleven men are women. There are actually a whole bunch more men and possibly a few women on each side. They stand on the sidelines, often in oversize parkas.

Tom Brady

Each team has a head coach whose job it is to yell at the players.

Even the players who are just wearing oversize parkas get yelled at. This happens when they get too close to the field. Coaches hate it when the players who aren't supposed to be in the game get too close to the field. They're supposed to know they aren't as good as the players on the field and stay the hell out of the way. Some teams even employ special coaches whose only job is to say, "Get back." They are the "get back" coaches. A referee can call a penalty if too many players are on the field, even if the extra player doesn't think he's not as good as the players who are on the field.

Head coaches at the highest level of tackle football, the National Football League, sometimes hold press conferences. The members of the media who attend are usually scared of the coaches and defer to them as though they were great heads of state. I didn't mean anything by that. Please don't yell at me. I'm wearing a parka. I'm way back of the sideline. Not even close to it. You are a very important man, sir. Coach. Big guy.

In Canada, they use twelve players on each side, exclusive of the players who aren't very good who wear parkas. They use twelve players in Canada because Canada has so much undeveloped land. It has so much undeveloped land that the United States used to use some of it to practice firing cruise missiles.

One time, the Raiders won a Super Bowl, and afterward, as I remember, President Reagan phoned the locker room (where did he get the phone number?) and ended up telling MVP Marcus Allen, "You are my cruise missile." Marcus didn't know what President Reagan was talking about. But President Reagan was somewhat prescient, if that's how you spell that word. It turned out Marcus Allen's brother, Damon, would play many years over Canada's still-undeveloped cruise-missile-testing land. In fact, he may still be playing up there.

I don't know if I used "prescient" the right way in that section on Canada. I was just trying to say that the Allens, Canada, Reagan, and cruise missiles were all related for some time. As great a man as President Reagan was, his funeral sure went on for a long time, didn't it? But enough about Canada.

In Canada there used to be two teams called the Rough Riders, though one of them may have been called the Roughriders. That was back when Canada had so many teams they ran out of names to call them. These days, there are about four or five CFL teams. They play each other ten or twelve times each during a season. I think they also play prison teams and college freshman teams, much like the schedules of junior college teams in the United States except that the junior college teams don't have to face Marcus Allen. He would absolutely crush my alma mater Wenatchee Valley Community College, he's so experienced.

He would except there is no tackle football team any longer at Wenatchee Valley Community College. There is no team at any junior or community college in Washington. None in Oregon either. The non–tackle football students got tired of seeing $49 of their $344 quarterly tuition go to a small minority of eighteen- and nineteen-year-olds who hadn't yet gotten tackle football completely out of their systems back in high school.

But it's too bad some alternative source of funding hasn't been found to keep junior or community college tackle football going. For some kids, tackle football is the only thing that keeps them going to school, even if it is just junior college. Many famous tackle football players played junior college tackle football. There's Hall of Fame tackle football quarterback Warren Moon, there's one of my best friends, receiver Jimmy Sandusky, and there's me.

My storied tackle football career began in my fifth-grade year. I tried to sign up in fourth grade but I wasn't old enough (nine instead of ten) and they told me to leave. I played soccer that season and gave up about eleven goals one day as the keeper. Somebody's mom gave us orange wedges afterward. Did she really think I could be bought off with orange wedges when it was tackle football I wanted to play? By the way, lady, the orange wedges had lots of seeds in them and weren't all that ripe. Make me some pudding.

Anyway, I had matured a lot by age ten and was accepted into the league. I weighed about forty-seven pounds. I had a very low body fat percentage.

I sucked and they never gave me the ball even though I was a running back. I was supposed to block people so the guy they kept giving the ball to, Mike Nelson, Susan Nelson's older brother, could run for glory. He wasn't getting much glory when he ran to my side of the formation, because I sucked at blocking too.

My goodness I loved tackle football.

I got to wear cool shoulder pads and a helmet and when my uniform got dirty that was great.

The next year I had filled out quite a bit. I weighed around fifty-seven pounds now. Wiry.

That's the year I had my femur snapped in half like a fresh carrot the day I tackled Keith Simons, who must have weighed about a gram under the weight limit for the "lightweight" (110-pound) division. Keith was carrying the ball in practice and I was coming up from my safety position to lay a big hit on him, just like Herb Adderly would have for my Packers. (They were my Packers because Seattle didn't have a team back then and Green Bay had won a couple of Super Bowls and what the hell, may as well back a winner, right?) Keith outweighed me about two to one and he also got lower than I did at the time of impact. His helmet drove my scrawny left leg over my head and I ended up on my back with my left leg in the position of my left arm had my left arm been asking a question. My question at that point was "How are we doing in this neighborhood as far as enhanced 911 goes?" I may not have really had that question in mind, for I was in shock. One of the coaches readjusted my left leg so that it was merely broken at the femur and no longer asking a question. They put me on some kind of wooden board stretcher and carried me to the back of coach Lyle Foltz's pickup truck. The other players piled their winter coats on top of me so I wouldn't go into shock even though I already had. So I was in shock, but fairly warm. Somebody stayed with me so I wouldn't feel lonely, I guess, while the rest of the players continued with practice. Somebody else got into a car because cell phones didn't exist. They were trying to find my parents so they could tell them I had tackled Keith Simons. Apparently they thought the people who lived across the street from the field where we were holding practice wouldn't let them use the phone. That would be asking a lot.

All I know is it started getting dark, practice ended, and a bunch of sixth-grade kids wanted their coats back—who cares if their teammate is going into shock? The little dorks starting pulling their coats off me and from under me, arguing about who had the black coat, who had the gray coat. I was bumped around in the back of Lyle Foltz's truck, in pain and in shock.

Did I mention I tackled Keith Simons?

Somebody finally located my parents, who immediately made a

worse decision than the one I'd made in not letting Keith Simons run free, and worse than the one to *not* call 911 or even an operator. And worse than the decision to *not* borrow a neighbor's phone. My parents had Lyle Foltz drive me to a local doctor's office instead of to a hospital. What the hell was he going to do for me? Give me a sticker?

I think he gave me morphine after making the incredibly astute observation that I'd broken my femur. Of course you break your femur when you weigh half as much as Keith Simons and try to tackle that big bastard.

Keith Simons now coaches tackle football at Santa Rosa Junior College in California, a state south of Washington where the non–tackle footballs students don't seem to care if forty-nine dollars of their tuition allows eighteen- and nineteen-year-olds to get football out of their systems. I'm certain Keith weighs more than 110 pounds now, but he hasn't, to the best of my knowledge, broken anyone else's femur.

The next year, I returned to the gridiron for more hard-hitting action. I was the quarterback. No more blocking for others. No more tackling Keith Simons (he was in the heavyweight division now). I think I threw about 23 passes all season. Mostly, my coach told me to hand the ball to his son and my best friend, Mark Sansaver. Mark gained about 2,000 yards on the ground. We never lost a game. I didn't break my femur. Some of the highlights of that season cannot be seen on ESPN Classic. I do have two nonaction still pictures. (One, with Mark Sansaver and me, is on the back of the book.)

In ninth grade, I was the second-string quarterback to Bruce Humphries, who was almost a full man already. I think he drove a Camaro to school. Mostly, I played in what was called "fifth quarter." This was for the awful players who hadn't made it into the real game, the one with four quarters. I think my dad was the only parent who watched fifth quarter. Poor bastard.

It was so humiliating to play in fifth quarter. I'd have preferred it if my dad had stayed at home, worked overtime, taken up crafts. Anything but standing and cheering me and the other parka wearers who hadn't played in the four lawful quarters of tackle football.

While we played in the extralegal fifth quarter, Bruce Humphries and the other starters did not stay to cheer us on. They turned their backs on the game to pick up cheerleaders, who weren't cheering for us.

Susan Nelson was one of the cheerleaders. I had my shot with her in seventh grade, but in seventh grade I was scared of girls. I'm still scared of girls. I had no shot with Susan Nelson by ninth grade. She came to the field each week to cheer her heart out for the guys who played in the first four quarters, not dorks like me, cover-boy nominees for *Parka Wear Quarterly*.

I do not remember a single play from any fifth-quarter game. If you call it a game. Screw fifth quarter.

I do remember one key play I made in a legal fourth quarter. And it almost counted for us. Coach Lou Blaise finally came to the realization around midseason that I could actually throw a football. I could throw even better than Bruce Humphries, even if Bruce had a better car than Lou Blaise. Coach had started using me to throw the ball in obvious passing situations. I'm no Bill Walsh, but down by five points with three seconds left to play, fourth down, 35 yards from the goal line sounds to me like an obvious passing situation. Coach Blaise looked at me and said, "Get in there and throw up a prayer."

We had no play called "throw up a prayer," plus Blaise didn't have as much confidence in me as I did. I knew I could throw the ball 40-odd yards in the air. I just needed time to do so. I told the linemen to block like they cared. I told Mark Sansaver to run a post route from the right flanker position and told the tight end, Lance Mihok, to run a post-corner to the right corner of the end zone. Mark drew the safety to the middle, Lance beat the kid trying to stay with him, and I heaved it to the right corner. Lance caught the ball. Even Susan Nelson had to notice.

I was a hero. Lance celebrated in the end zone, the cheerleaders almost cheered, my dad acted like the dad of the quarterback who had just thrown the game winner.

Then one of the men officiating the game signaled (quite late) that the pass had been caught out of bounds.

It was a terrible call. Lance was definitely in bounds. If you don't believe me, call Lance right now. His number is 212-782-9127.

The week after my near heroics, I broke my leg again. Coach Blaise was actually going to give me the start in the next game. In practice that Wednesday, however, I was running opposition plays for our first-team defense. They were taking turns sacking me. It was Fred George's turn. He dove at my left ankle. It snapped.

Coaching had improved since sixth grade. Lou Blaise called 911.

I don't remember much about my high school tackle football years except that we were always third best when the season ended and only the top two made the state tackle football playoffs. I do remember being named the Player of the Week by one of the Seattle papers (Joe Orr and Mark Sansaver had big games that night too). The guy from the paper wildly misquoted me in his story. I haven't trusted the mainstream media since.

In junior college I was picked off four times in the same game. We were playing at Columbia Basin, down there near the Columbia Basin. My roommate, a Canadian named John McKay, who looked even older than Bruce Humphries had in junior high, and who could buy beer, was supposed to have been blocking for me in his running back position. Just after he was knocked down, I was picked off. I made some kind of half-assed attempt to chase down the defensive back who was running for a touchdown. John just lay on the field. But later on film, we did notice his extraordinary effort. He was seen pretending to shoot the guy from the other team who was returning the pick for a touchdown.

I made honorable mention All-America in my second junior college season. So did about twenty other quarterbacks. Like me, most of them probably now just say "All-America quarterback" when recounting their junior college years, leaving out the honorable-mention part.

I was not All-America at UNLV. I was barely at UNLV. I was the second-string quarterback my junior year to a guy named Larry Gentry. I was the second-string quarterback my senior year to a guy named Sam King. It is often misreported, but since it's really my only athletic bragging point (besides throwing out Ozzie Smith going to third in Legends-Celebrity softball on ESPN in 2007) I think it's fair to note. I was *ahead of, not behind* Randall Cunningham on the 1981 UNLV depth chart. A guy named Allyn Reynolds (third string) can still say the same thing.

In my junior season, 1980, I was just starting to play a bit more in the games when we flew to Eugene, Oregon, to play the Ducks. We were getting trashed, something like 33–9. It was down to the last play of the game. I called "go" routes for the wide receivers and figured we'd at least take one more shot at putting some more points on the board. The pass fell incomplete. I fell to the ground. Broken. The left defensive end for Oregon had put his helmet on my right ankle. Not the same ankle Fred George had fractured in ninth grade, or the ankle below the femur Keith Simons had fractured in sixth grade. No, this was a brand-new experience for me. This time, my ankle was both fractured *and* dislocated. Bonus. The bone was broken and every ligament in the neighborhood was shredded. It felt like my leg was underground. Mr. Foltz wasn't there to put me in his pickup truck. None of the Oregon players offered me a winter coat. It was just me and my leg. Underground.

My right ankle and toe have been operated on seven times since that play. My right ankle is sitting under a bag of ice as I write this. And I still love tackle football. What do four billion people know?

After my senior year at UNLV, my coach there, Tony Knapp, talked the Seahawks into giving me a tryout when Sam King turned down their free-agent deal to go to sign in Canada. He probably went there because of all that undeveloped land.

I flew to Seattle and threw for their quarterbacks coach, Jerry Rhome. Afterward, he told the player personnel director, Dick Mansberger, that I wasn't "terrible."

Either the Seahawks had lowered their standards, or they needed more bodies for the potential strike that year (there was one). Whatever the case, I was offered a contract for thirty thousand dollars with raises *all the way to forty-five thousand dollars.* I got to work out with the team at its old Kirkland, Washington, headquarters, on the shore of Lake Washington. (The part about "the shore of Lake Washington" wasn't all that necessary, but this is my first book, and in case I end up doing Great American Novels one day, I'll need to work on my scene settings.) During those workouts, my confidence was buoyed when Seattle fullback Dan Doornink, who was even bigger than Keith Simons, saw me complete a 22-yard "out" route. He said to me, "If you can throw that route, you can throw anything." It was the nicest thing anyone has ever said about me.

I didn't really think I was going to unseat the Seattle starter, Jim Zorn, or his backup, Dave Krieg, who was from tiny Milton College, which no longer exists (see "Bowling"). I just wanted to last long enough for somebody to notice me, even Susan Nelson. Maybe I would get a shot in the upstart USFL or, really now, Canada. Some of my best games were played on undeveloped land.

But on the first day of official training camp in Cheney, Washington, they put me through one last check of my ankle. I failed miser-

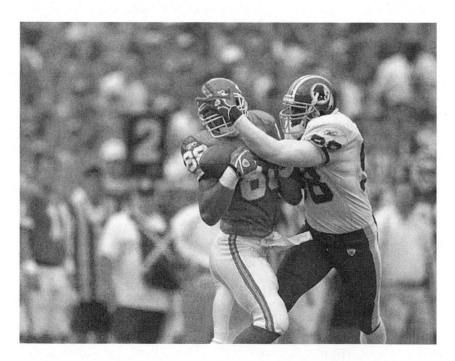

Some NFL contests deteriorate into a game of peekaboo.

ably on the Cybex machine. Had I known it was to test the strength of my bad ankle, and not just some random fitness test (which I naively thought it was), I would have cheated. I would have gone easy on my good left ankle and pushed my right (bad) ankle like I was trying to fool trained physicians. Instead, I pushed both equally hard and my right leg came up deficient. The machine spit out some kind of graph info like a lie-detector test.

My right ankle had lied.

The Seahawks had an intern drive me to the Spokane airport in a team van. He handed me ten dollars for airport meal money, the last dollar in quarters.

I now play tackle football only with my daughters other than when I throw with my NFL features producer, Tom McCollum, at NFL training sites. Lambeau Field was our biggest thrill. Tom is way better than some of those fifth-quarter players from Totem Junior High.

Recently, when my contract with ESPN came up for renewal, and our family's situation was up in the air, my older daughter, Riley, said, "Maybe you should consider playing professional football." It was the nicest thing anyone has ever said about me.

That's pretty much all, or at least all the important stuff you need to know about tackle football, except that my wife, Laura, has always been sort of attracted to Joe Montana. Joe's won four Super Bowls. Three times he was the Super Bowl MVP. He's in the Hall of Fame. He was All-America at Notre Dame. He was *Sports Illustrated*'s Man of the Year. He's married to a former model.

I am attracted to Joe Montana.

> Tackle football is my favorite sport, so this fact better be pretty good.
> Despite spending his first six pro seasons in Canada, Warren Moon ranked third all time in NFL passing yardage and fourth in touchdown passes at the time of his retirement.

Tackle Football:
Fake Punt, Sucker

If this looks like another tackle football chapter, it is.

One day, a long time ago, Washington State was playing Oregon.

Years later I would break my leg at Oregon, so it's good somebody did something bad to the people of Oregon.

Washington State playing Oregon was significant to my family even though we lived south of Seattle and should have been Washington fans. My sister Leslie dated Ty Paine, the quarterback at Washington State in the late sixties and early seventies.

He wasn't involved in this play but he later drew it up for me. It looked something like this.

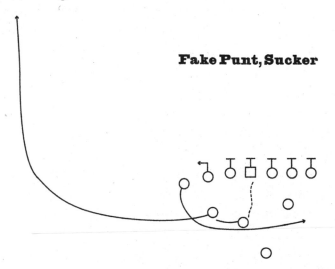

Fake Punt, Sucker

The Cougars were lined up to punt. But they didn't. Otherwise the name of the play would have been just "punt." In truth, when punters are in the huddle, they don't actually call "punt" as the play, just as field goal kickers don't call out "field goal" as the play. Everyone knows why they are out there at that point in the game. The only need for a call is when they are not going to kick it, as in, "fake punt, sucker."

The ball was snapped to the punter's personal protector. He then stuck the ball between the legs of Bernard Jackson, a great runner who would later play defensive back for the Broncos. Jackson was lined up to the left of the personal protector, in position to act as another blocking back for the punter, whose name escapes me right now, but what does it matter, he didn't even touch the ball on the play.

The guy who put the ball between Bernard Jackson's legs then pretended to give the ball to some other guy who ran from the end of the line on the left side behind the guy who had put the ball between Jackson's legs and toward the right side of the formation. All the players on the Washington State sideline started yelling, "Reverse! Reverse!" The punter, who never touched the ball, not even to stick it between Bernard Jackson's legs, then pretended to punt the ball, which he didn't have.

A guy on Oregon, if that's who Washington State was even playing, I'm mixed up at this point, ran up to Bernard and actually put his hands on Jackson's shoulder pads. He shoved Jackson to the side and began pursuing the guy who didn't have the ball who had started the play on the left end of the line of scrimmage but who was now running without the ball to the right side of the field.

Bernard still had the ball between his legs while everyone else on the field was either faking they had or used to have the ball or faking that they were punting the ball which they never had.

At this point, Bernard Jackson took the ball out from between his legs and started running. He ran down the left sideline and into the end zone for a touchdown. I have no idea who won the game and I don't want to throw off my momentum looking it up. It's easily found on the Internet. The Internet has everything. Some of it is even true.

Fake story, sucker.

That was just a way to end the story. But it was the wrong way. It is a true story except for the parts I sort of made up.

But truly. A ball was snapped to one guy, who put it between the legs of another guy. The guy who put it between the other guy's legs then faked that he still had the ball and faked further that he was giving the ball he didn't have to another guy who never had the ball and never had a chance at touching the ball unless he wanted to take it from the guy who had the ball between his legs. That would have been stupid. It would have blown the entire plan.

I don't think I saw the play. I heard it on the radio. Great call by Bob Robertson, if that's the guy who made the call. If not, Bob would have loved that play. I know I did.

Fake story, sucker.

That's what you expected again. But no. It really happened. You can look it up. It really happened. I can see it so vividly. Not on the radio. On the TV show the day after the game. They used to have a show where the coach (Jim Sweeney) would come on and talk about the game. He must have had a lot to talk about that Sunday.

Either way, it really happened. It was a much better day than the time my family flew to Los Angeles (my dad worked for United and we could fly to L.A. for about thirty dollars as a family) to see Washington State try a bunch of other plays that didn't work very well. You can look it up. It was like 1969. Or maybe it was 1970. How am I supposed to remember? I was either nine or ten years old. Maybe I was eleven. No. That couldn't be. I broke my leg when I was eleven. Maybe you've heard about it. Keith Simons weighed about 340 pounds back then. Why did they put me in a pickup truck when they should have put me in an ambulance?

What a bunch of idiots. I don't remember what year it was when we went to L.A. and Washington State sucked. I know what year it is right now. I don't mean right now. I mean when the book comes out. Then again, if you bought the book the year after it came out it would be a different year. Why are you asking so many questions? What if you stole the book? Was it worth it, now that you've read this crap? That would be: fake purchase, sucker. That would be bad. But not as bad as that Oregon guy who broke my right ankle. It hurts right now. How bad do you think the other Oregon guy felt when he found out he had put his hands on Bernard Jackson but not tackled him? I wonder what he's doing now. I don't mean right now. It's about 9:08 p.m. eastern where I am. I don't even know where he lives. Now it's 9:09. I didn't get very far in that one minute, did I? Bet you're glad you stole the book and didn't waste any money.

Fake last part of chapter, sucker.

> Here is a sports fact not quite as good as the one about Warren Moon, but still a real sports fact.
>
> Wilson began making the official NFL game ball in 1941. Footballs are to be inflated to thirteen pounds of pressure.

Tackle Football: Randall Cunningham

Randall Cunningham isn't really a sport. But then, is this really a book about sports? I'm sitting on a plane to Los Angeles in February of 2007 (my, how the literary world moves with haste). I'm on the way to cover a story about Santa Anita jockeys playing basketball against eighth graders for charity. If I'm doing that for an all-sports network, I can make Randall Cunningham a sport in my book.

In my senior year at UNLV, Sam King was the starter. I was second string. Allyn Reynolds was third. And a freshman kid out of Santa Barbara, Randall Cunningham, was fourth string.

Randall was like a big puppy. He was six feet four inches but seemed to be seven feet tall. He was too cocky for our tastes at times but in those times we would remind him that he was fourth string. After practice, we would warm down our arms with some light tosses at ten yards. Sam King, the smartest of us, would walk to the locker room. The rest of us would risk arm injury by then holding a contest to see who could throw the farthest, with the gym building being our target. Allyn would top out at about sixty yards or so. I could launch the ball somewhere past seventy yards, same as redshirt quarterback Steve White. Randall was in the eighties. As he used to say, I ain't lyin'.

Sometimes we would throw all at once. That was even more demoralizing. Randall's ball was still climbing as ours were in descent to earth.

So we knew the guy was an athlete. He just didn't have the somewhat complicated offense down yet. As a matter of fact, only Sam King did. (Sam was 255-433 for a school record 3,778 yards passing in 1981.)

It was preordained that Randall would make it to the NFL. His brother, Sam Cunningham, played in the league for nine seasons. Randall was a star. And funny. It won't be funny now, but it's my story. Or it may be to the select few who can recall a television commercial from the 1970s for 3 Musketeers candy bars. The lame ad spoke of how fluffy the bar was, how it could just float away. "There goes my bar." One day after practice Randall was holding a 3 Musketeers bar and he pretended it was starting to float away from him. He extended one of his five-foot-long arms and said, "There goes my bar."

Told you it might not be funny now.

I wish he'd said that much to me in the fall of 1989. By then he had been labeled the "Ultimate Weapon" by *Sports Illustrated.* By then, I had quit my Seattle TV job on one day's notice. This was just after interviewing for, but not winning, a TV job at ESPN. I didn't have much money in savings, but I pretty much went "all in" (and borrowed a little from my sister Leslie) to try to win over ESPN right then and there. I flew to Philadelphia, hired a camera crew, and sought to do the definitive feature on my old friend and teammate, superstar Randall Cunningham.

There goes my story.

My thought was I'd impress ESPN so much with this up-close story with one of the league's stars that I'd overcome whatever it was they hadn't liked about me in the interview six months previous. This would be the nudge to have them offer me a full-time position.

I sent word to Randall through his Eagles public relations department that I'd be coming to the game against the Giants that Sunday. I figured it was a lock that I'd get fifteen to twenty minutes alone with Randall after the game, a favor from an old friend and

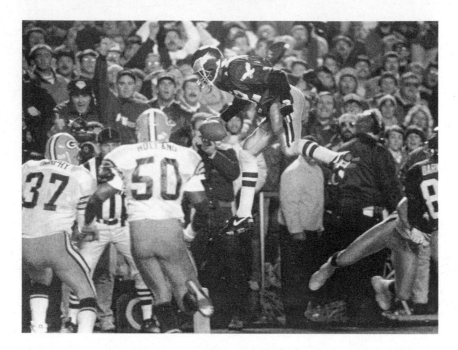

*We couldn't find a photograph of his touchdown against the Giants . . .
but this is pretty good.*

teammate that would save my career. The Eagles beat the Giants
and Randall had a huge game. It was all lining up favorably for my
job-creation plan. This was the game where Randall scored a
touchdown on one of his more famous head-over-heels dives at the
goal line.

I crossed paths with Randall as he entered the general press conference, the one for all the media members who hadn't played tackle
football with him in college. I quickly explained to him what I was
up to and he responded, "Sorry, man. I have to be somewhere right
after this is over."

There goes my job.

As I sat listening to his generic answers to generic questions about
this particular game against the Giants, the weight of it all sank in. I
had quit a job that was going well six months previous, because of a
dispute with The Man, and now I was going to be completely broke

after betting the last of what I had on a relationship that wasn't as deep as I'd thought it was. I was just one more reporter in the room, asking the Ultimate Weapon some ultimately unimportant questions. There was no close-up to be had. No one on one.

There was Randall leaving the room, heading outside, not seeing me, or maybe ignoring me giving chase. He got into a long stretch limousine. These were the days of long stretch limos for Randall, and gold-laced shoulder pads.

There goes my friend.

Now it's 1998. Randall has returned to being the guy whose fluffy candy bar is floating away. The ego has floated away too. Funny how that could be, as he's leading the Vikings to the then all-time team scoring record in a season. (How did they not win the Super Bowl?)

Two years previous, my wife, Laura, and I had lost twin sons, Creighton and Connor. They were born at twenty-three weeks, four days. Creighton died at birth. Connor lived for six months.

I met with Randall in the Vikings' lunchroom after practice. His arms were still long. But we were closer again. He had turned (or maybe returned) to Christianity. He wore his belief on his long sleeve. The same people who criticized him for his selfishness in Philadelphia were on him now for his announced selflessness. But I was there to experience the truth of it.

He had heard about our sons but wanted to know the whole story. I went on and on about Connor's courage in the hospital, how his mom stayed with him for twenty hours at a time. Randall just listened, respectfully. He was clearly saddened by all this but displayed a confidence about what was in store. He mentioned something about how we'll never really understand on earth how God works, how we must simply accept what's dealt us, as hard as that is. Laura and I were pretty well set with that manner of thinking. One either goes on, or doesn't.

Randall asked if it would be okay if he and his team pastor, Keith Johnson, say a prayer for our family.

The three of us retreated to an unused office space off the lunchroom. It was there that Keith Johnson told God what's what. It wasn't the kind of prayer I was used to making. Mine were more about general inquiries as to whether this or that might happen for me or another.

Keith Johnson went fire and brimstone on God. He demanded. Demanded that our family be blessed with a healthy child. Now.

I thanked them both, and returned home to tell Laura about the prayer. She was very moved and thankful. We had suffered two miscarriages since losing the boys. Many of our days were dark.

Laura loved the extra help, but she informed me that God's intervention would likely have to wait another month or two. She had the same command of her ovulation figures as NASA has of the heavens before a shuttle launch. The stars and her ovaries were not aligned to make a baby anytime soon.

Two weeks later, we went to Vermont to go skiing. Just before heading out the door, Laura said she wanted to do a pregnancy test, "even though there's no shot we are pregnant." After all the losses, she didn't want to take any chances with the health of a new baby.

The test was positive.

The baby born is Riley *Hope* Mayne.

Her picture of Randall Cunningham is to the right.

There goes his bar.

He raised it.

Here is an interesting and relevant fact.

Randall Cunningham is one of only five quarterbacks in NFL history with 25,000 career passing yards and 3,000 career rushing yards.

Team Handball

Team handball has nothing to do with the kind of handball that the fellas play in New York City up against graffiti-covered walls. Or the kind business executives play against white walls over three-hour lunches. Team handball is something else entirely.

What exactly, I have no idea.

The one time I saw it was a time from long ago.

It was the Goodwill Games of 1990.

That was the sporting competition meant to bring about goodwill.

I was busy trying to foster goodwill with ESPN. The network had called to offer me a reporting position for the Games, which were being held in Seattle. Since I lived in Seattle, this was an easy decision for ESPN. They didn't have to send anyone from Connecticut to cover an event no one knew was taking place.

I was busy trying to find rhythmic gymnastics and instead ran smack into team handball. Anyone knows what rhythmic gymnastics is or are? That's the sport in which a bunch of girls in leotards run around with paper streamers and get points from judges.

Team handball? No clue. Not me. I think it involves teams. Probably two of them.

There are probably so many players on each team there's simply no way to fit them all safely inside a regular handball court. Plus, with those business execs taking three-hour lunches, the team handball teams always get screwed on court space.

It would be murder if the team handball guys tried to play on a handball court *and* share space with the rhythmic gymnasts. Plus the team handball guys would get tangled up in those paper streamers, since they're not very practiced in working with paper streamers, being team handball guys and all.

For team handball players to share space with rhythmic gymnasts it would be just like back in junior high when the phys ed teachers used to pull that partition across the gym floor so that the boys could play dodgeball while the girls did who knows what, probably sex ed. Whatever sex ed is about.

In team handball, as far as I could tell, a bunch of men run around on a rhythmic gymnastics floor and throw a small ball to each other. The goal is to throw the ball to each other until one of the players throws it in a more important place.

Then the team handball crowd goes nuts.

It looked like a great way to get in shape, and look at all the good-will that was fostered from this. It took only four more years for me to get a job at ESPN. It's surprising they haven't had me cover more team handball.

Here is a fact.

Team handball might be something of a combination of basketball and soccer but I wasn't really paying that much attention.

Tennis

Tennis used to be better when John McEnroe was yelling all the time.

You cannot be serious.

No. I am.

Answer the question.

The question, jerk.

Here's what I got out of all that. The words were memorable, but the meaning was deeper. John McEnroe was telling me, a college student, watching him take on Borg and Connors *and authority,* that it's okay to stand up for oneself. Even if doing so is injurious.

Essentially, what he was saying is it's okay to protest the injustices set upon us by totalitarians who seek to emasculate us with their rules and their rigidity, their indifference to individualism, their closed-mindedness.

Also, he was saying, "The ball was in."

It was the summer of '79. I was getting ready for my first tackle football season at UNLV. I would have been ready except that I cut two tendons in my middle (throwing) finger about a week before practice started. But before that, I was ready to take on all challenges. I was not going to take no for an answer. I was doing all that partly because I had been watching John McEnroe at Wimbledon.

What McEnroe was telling me and anyone who would listen is that it's cool to stand up for yourself. It's not only that, it is your right. Now there are some more diplomatic ways to do it. But in the heat of the battle, when what matters most to you is entirely in the balance, it is your right, your duty even, to give every ounce of energy, to give your heart, your spirit, your forehand and backhand, to succeeding at the very thing you've worked so hard to accomplish.

McEnroe was childish. He was disrespectful. He was out of control. He was my role model.

Whether he would win or lose the argument as to just where the ball had landed was immaterial. The lesson I learned is that there is victory in simply putting the argument out there into the universe. You may be outnumbered or outranked, but you will be justified for making certain that everyone watching and listening hears the truth (or the exercise of your right to express your version of it).

Mostly, he was honest. He may have been wrong at times. Maybe he didn't have the best view of where the ball had landed. But he believed passionately in what he thought he saw. He didn't simply lash out only at others. He faulted himself when he thought he was the jerk. He yelled at himself when he misplayed or miscalculated. He yelled at the chair when a call didn't but should have gone his way. He yelled also when the call didn't and shouldn't have gone his way. But on those occasions he wasn't being dishonest. He just didn't have all the information. On those occasions, with the replay equipment he now employs as an analyst, he would have yelled at himself for being so wrong.

That has to be the case. Otherwise *he could not be serious.* He could not be that rebel model that he was to many of us. Those of us who fed off his energy wanted him to be right all the time. But mostly, we stole some of his energy, some of his attitude, and applied it to our lives.

This had nothing to do with tennis. He had nothing to do with tennis for me. If he regrets any of the behavior, that's his loss. The attitude and passion he exhibited crossed way over any tennis line, to be applied in any arena of life, in any passionate fight.

We wanted to go out and get what it was we desired and in doing so make certain that even if we failed in the pursuit, the truth would always be held paramount.

Answer the question, jerks.

> This is a sports fact.
>
> John McEnroe and Bjorn Borg split their fourteen head-to-head matches between 1978 and 1981. McEnroe won three of the four grand slam finals they were in together.

Tetherball

Tetherball is a game played in fifth or sixth grade and then it is never played again.

In fact, after fifth or sixth grade, unless you are a volunteer parent at your local elementary, you will never see tetherball again.

In tetherball, a ball is "tethered" to a rope and a rope is "tethered" to a metal pole. Two players try to slap the ball in opposite directions until the ball wraps around the metal pole, or until one of the players gets tangled up in the tether, or until the ball goes flying over to the kickball field, it being no longer very tethered.

Sometimes means kids come by and rip the ball out of its tethered relationship to the tethered rope and punt it into the woods. At that point, the game is over.

Tetherball has not been recognized as an Olympic sport.

As I write this, the Colts just beat the Ravens in an American Football Conference playoff game. This is a good point of reference for you with regard to what I was just thinking about.

I have never seen a tetherball game played since I was in sixth grade.

In sixth grade, I had the opportunity to be the safety patrol captain. I turned down the job because I knew I didn't want to get up an extra forty-five minutes early each day to stand in the rain. I also knew I wasn't responsible enough.

By passing on that opportunity, I had plenty of energy for competing in tetherball action.

This was a stupid chapter.

> But it can be saved with a great sports fact.
>
> Tetherball is considered a "playground activity" and not an official sport. Therefore, it is not even governed by official rules for play. What the heck kind of sport is this doing in my book?

Track and Field

There are about forty different events in track and field but the coolest one by far is the men's 100 meters.

The winner of that, in the World Games and/or in the Olympics, is called "the world's fastest man."

It's a little like how our NBA title team is called "world champion" when only the United States and Canada compete for the NBA title (see "Basketball"). I say this because, with respect to the 100 meters, we may crown a guy who runs a 9.74 the world's fastest man, but there could easily be some undiscovered guy in Lesotho who can run a 9.73. He just hasn't been discovered or cannot afford track shoes or doesn't have a track team. It's like Chris Rock's line, "They pay me for the jokes *I don't tell.*"

I don't know for sure everything I meant by that, but I agree with Chris Rock when at the Oscars he said there are only a few real stars—the rest are just famous. I don't know for sure if that was the actual quote, which is why I didn't use quote marks. Plus, to use quote marks, you have to readjust your fingers on the keyboard. Right now I'm killing myself trying to rewrite this book, and I cannot put any more stress on my fingers. This is why I'm not even going to finish this se

In the men's 100 meters, the guys are very fast.

They are way faster than I was in junior college and ran the 400 meters. I knew that I had no shot at being named world's fastest man right after I signed up for the 400 meters. They hand out the world's fastest man title only to those in the 100 meters.

The reason I entered any kind of racing event was to get in shape for the next season of tackle football. You'd think there would have been a less taxing way to do this. The tackle football coaches wanted me to work on my speed for the next tackle football season. They probably wanted me to do this so I wouldn't end up on a street corner drinking wine from a paper sack and so that when I was intercepted a bunch of times the next season, I'd have the necessary speed to run down the defensive back who was running for a touchdown. He must have been real tired having to drop back in pass coverage, intercept my pass, and run the long distance to the other goal line. I wonder if he was as tired as I am right now, typing my ass off to get this book finished.

In addition to not having any chance at being named world's fastest man, I had no shot at being named race's fastest man in the 400 meters. This is mostly due to the fact that I wasn't very fast.

But for me, with my generic 4.7 40 speed, I actually acquitted myself fairly well in track and field, though I spent no time in the field. There was no way I was going to pick up one of those stupid shots. They weigh like eight pounds, way heavier than a football, which really has no set weight. It's just supposed to be inflated to thirteen pounds of pressure.

What was Chris Rock saying again?

But back to the 40 time thing. I've always wondered why tackle football coaches make such a big production of the 40 time. Besides the fact that there is a great variance in how well coaches time all these 40s, when is the last time you saw a tackle football game stopped so everyone could be timed in a 40?

My first attempt to run a 400-meter race against actual collegiate competition came in the spring of 1978 at Bellevue Community College. It was an all-comers meet, which explained why I was allowed to run. There were half a dozen colleges there. For some reason actual men from the University of Washington showed up to race against community colleges and the slow people like me the community colleges had sent over.

I drew lane 8 for my maiden race, which gave me a great head start (the start positions are staggered so that each runner ends up running the same distance). I carried my "lead" into the turn for home and in my peripheral vision, if that's how you spell "vision," I saw no one. Right then I was a little worried about my peripheral vision. But mostly, I was astonished at this new speed I had acquired. These were real track-and-field guys out there running, not a bunch of quarterbacks trying to improve their 40 time. By the way, if my coaches were so worried about my 40 time, why did they have me running 400 meters all the time? Maybe it was the thing about the wine from a paper sack that they were most concerned with.

With no one in sight, I was fairly certain I was going to win a 400-meter race in my first attempt.

My grandma Mayne lived about a block from the track. My father and she walked over to watch the race. I thought about them when I turned for home. I thought about them right after I thought about how there might be something wrong with my peripheral vision. Then my peripheral vision was restored. I saw *seven* other runners running much faster than me. One by one these faster runners ran faster than me. Then they passed me. The people holding the tape at the finish line seemed to be running the other way. The 400 meters felt like it was now a 500- or 600-meter race. The oxygen in my legs was totally depleted. I was going very slowly. I was in eighth place. I got my ass kicked by seven actual track-and-field runners. There is no way anyone went away saying, "That guy in eighth place is the fastest man in the world."

Just past the finish line this thought crossed my mind: "Am I having a heart attack?"

I continued to run the 400 meters to improve my 40 time and stop drinking so much wine from paper bags. Getting in shape for tackle football season meant that much to me. It meant so much to me that I would go out each week and have seven other runners run way faster than me. Slow as I was, I found one runner even slower. I once finished in *seventh* out of eight runners. I wonder what that guy is doing right now.

Probably something very slow.

Years later I wonder: Why didn't I just run 40s to improve my 40 time?

Here's a sports fact way better than that last pile of crap about tetherball, which isn't even a sport.

Nine-time Olympic gold medalist Carl Lewis didn't play basketball or football in college but he was a tenth-round draft pick of the Chicago Bulls and a twelfth-round pick of the Dallas Cowboys in 1984. He played for neither.

Third and Final Time-out

Wiffle Ball

Wiffle ball is the second-greatest game in the world next to tackle football and everyone knows it.

We played our games at Alma Memorial, the field on the upper portion of my parents' property. It was named for my grandma, Alma Creighton. She died in 1976. Before that time we were just playing on the upper portion of my parents' property. It would have been mean to have called the field Alma Memorial before she died. I'm still sad she died and wish we were still playing on a field called "the upper portion of my parents' property." But if that were the case, she would be 114 years old. I think I mentioned this in my baseball chapter, but I wrote that about three hours ago. My friend,

Mark Sansaver, broke Babe Ruth's home run record before Henry Aaron did.

I don't remember the year, but it was memorable.

The year was 1972. We kept statistics on every game. I was in charge of keeping them. I have no idea where the stats are now. I was just in charge of keeping them. Not saving them. Anyway, for every game, pretty much every day in spring and summer, I noted who did what so that years later (like this year) we could reflect on that great year, 1972. Given the fact the stats are lost, long-term memory will have to suffice. This is pretty much how the guys at the Elias Sports Bureau do their thing.

The only stats that should count, if they could be found, are the ones played in games using the official skinny yellow Wiffle ball bat.

I do not like it when people spell Wiffle ball as Whiffle ball, with the extra *h*. It would seem that an *h* is appropriate, and I just saw the *New York Times* add an *h*, but that's not how the guys from Shelton, Connecticut, spelled it when they sat down one day and designed the game.

Wiffle Ball Guy: Let's manufacture a skinny yellow bat and two sizes of plastic balls with holes in them and see if kids will play a form of baseball, called Wiffle ball.

Other Wiffle Ball Guy: Shouldn't we spell it with an *h*?

My dad's dad owned a hardware store. He was as handy as handy could be. There was a big handy as handy could be regression in the genes passed down to my father. He was a lot less handy as handy can be. But he did manage to build us a killer outfield fence for our Wiffle ball at Alma Memorial. The fence made the home runs seem so much more official. The regression in handy as handy can be skills was even more severe when the genes were handed out to me. I need instructions to work a Phillips screwdriver. (A comic on HBO first said something like that.)

When my sister Carolee was home, we'd drag her up to Alma so she could perform the national anthem. If we had fireworks handy (as handy can be) we'd light those off just about the time Carolee hit "home of the brave." She'd then take off to do whatever sisters do and we'd start the action. Six, seven hours of action. Two on two, three on three. Whoever could be there was in the game. We'd make all the phone calls to the usual suspects. There were the Sansavers, Mark and Bruno; the Dorans, Shawn and Dennis; Dave LeClair; Kurt Essman; Mike McCauley; and Mike Miller. Jeff Whidden lived two doors down. Mike Smith would ride his bike down the hill from Cambridge. Scott Lennox was a great lefty. Sometimes the paperboy, Phil Henry, took the field. Other times, when we already had even numbers, Phil would umpire. Years later, he accosted Mark Sansaver at a party and alleged that Mark was in on some kind of conspiracy to make Phil Henry have to umpire all the time. It wasn't true. Who-ever was odd man upon arrival had to ump before he could play. We all took turns. On even-numbered games, pitcher's decisions ruled.

Mark hit 843 home runs that year. Thirty were later discounted. Those home runs came off an illegal "fat bat." We regretted ever using the fat bats, and are shamed to this day, but sometimes the skinny yellow bats were lost or broken. We wanted to play but were fresh out of official equipment and my sister Nancy wasn't home to drive us to Valu-Mart to restock. So to play at all, we went to the backup bat, the fat bat. I am shamed.

Alma Memorial had more ground rules than I can remember. In recalling some now, I don't see the intention of all those rules.

A ball that was hit into the bushes on the left side of the field could bounce or roll back into play and be considered fair, while a ball that even skimmed a bush or a tree branch on the right side of the field was out of play.

In looking through the chapters of this book, I don't see the inten-tion behind the inclusion of some.

The field was narrow and the pitching mound was about thirty feet from home plate. It was a gentlemen's game with regard to pitching speed. The rule was that pitchers had to throw "medium" speed. Many arguments took place.

Home plate was a stolen street sign, a very big stop sign. (I didn't do it. One of the senior, exhibition-game participants, my sister's boyfriend Matt McGillen, did the crime.) (He was a good guy otherwise and, in fact, a literary mentor.) Using the very wide strike zone, due to the use of the stolen stop sign, made for a lot of defensive games.

It was all the more laudable then that Mark Sansaver hit 843 home runs (officially: 813).

The day Mark went past Babe Ruth for number 715 was a moment we will all cherish forever. We would cherish it forever if only we could remember how we noted it, or when it happened. Or who was there that day. I think after Mark hit that home run I went down to the house and wrote up a fake newspaper article about it.

That's been lost too.

But never have I lost the feeling of what it was to take the field. It was always better when I had an odd number of friends, because then no one had to ump. We lined the field with sugar. We stood for

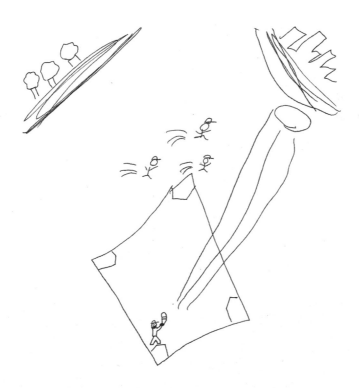

the anthem. We argued over whether the ball had touched a leaf, whether the pitcher's "medium" was really a fastball.

That field could still be called the upper portion of my parents' property. It could be if only Alma Creighton were 114 years old. And if only my parents hadn't sold the property.

But memories aren't for sale. Nor are the memorable records.

Here is a somewhat relevant fact about Wiffle ball.

The stats are lost now, but I think we all gave up home runs to Mark Sansaver. That said, the only two pitchers to give up home runs to both Barry Bonds and Hank Aaron were Rick Reuschel and Frank Tanana.

Wiffle Ball: Haunted by Ghost Runners

We were purists. I mean, we even knew Wiffle ball had no *h* in it. We knew we were playing damn near every day, every summer.

Each Wiffle ball field had its own unique ground rules. At the Whiddens' house, two doors down, a ball hit into the lake on the fly was a home run, into the lake on one bounce, a triple, and so on. Always, it was "pitcher's hand" for an out on the lead runner.

Ghost runners were made necessary on many of the fields due to limitations of space. But at my parents' house, the most sacred park in the Wiffle ball solar system we traveled in the 1960s and '70s, who needed a ghost runner when we had Mark Sansaver?

Thirty years later, it is Mark who could use a ghost runner.

Mark and his family had moved to the Seattle area (about eight doors down from us) when he was ten years old. Ten was the number of children in that family, all of them athletic, well-muscled. Mark was the youngest boy and showed the most athletic potential.

His speed was legendary at Star Lake Elementary, for he was the only true rival to Terese Rehfeldt when it came time to run the 30-yard dash during the President's Council on Physical Fitness test. Terese was pretty. And she was pretty damn fast.

Thirty years later, the precise memory is unclear as to whether Mark really beat Terese. Maybe through the Freedom of Information Act, I could force the federal government to reveal the official record on the speed figures from 1969. Maybe it's all on paper somewhere in our permanent records.

I do remember being an awkward ten-year-old, all hands and feet, yet at the same time appreciative of the true physical talent possessed by my classmates.

Just before flying to Seattle for baseball's All-Star event in July 2001, I called Montana to check on how Mark was doing with his muscular dystrophy. His wife, Kelli, while trying to remain positive, imparted the harsh truth. Mark now needs braces much of the time to support his deteriorating muscles. There's no guarantee he'll end up in a wheelchair like his brother Bill Jr. But there's no cure either.

Kelli spoke of the emotional toll: Mark's contemplation of the fact that he isn't (physically) the same man she married seventeen years ago, not the exact same person who fathered three wonderful girls (none has signs of the disease). He's not the same physical specimen who played college football, and he's no longer the ten-year-old who challenged Terese Rehfeldt on a cement playground, as the rest of us stood in awe.

By some curious confluence of fate in the span of a few July days, I would speak with Mark's wife about his MD, I would stand on the Whiddens' Wiffle ball field (they call it a yard these days) and light off fireworks on the Fourth of July, carrying the last of my father's ashes (his wish), and I would meet with some old high school friends in Seattle the night before the All-Star Game. One of them would be Terese Rehfeldt, now a mother of three. I've known her since kindergarten, but I hadn't seen her since high school.

The morning of the All-Star Game, I interviewed Dale Earnhardt Jr., who has nothing to do with baseball except for the fact that he drives for Budweiser and beer fuels baseball. As we concluded, Earnhardt Jr.'s PR man said, "If there's anything we can ever do for you . . ."

And I said, "As a matter of fact . . ."

My sister Leslie works for the Muscular Dystrophy Association and had asked me the night before about the remote chance of landing a couple tickets for the sold-out game. She was hoping to help twelve-year-old Josh Hope, who is confined to a wheelchair. She told me she knew there'd be little chance at this point to get the tickets. She did not know that PR men, particularly PR men for beer companies, always have extra tickets.

Nor did she know that a friend on the Mariners' staff would lead me to a good man in the ticketing department who would turn that pair of 300-level tickets into 100-level tickets directly behind home plate.

Josh and his mother, Bambi, had just been given an eviction notice (of less than thirty days, the bastards) to vacate her rented home. (That eviction notice was later rescinded.) Muscular dystrophy or not, they deserved home plate tickets as much as anyone.

During pregame ceremonies I sought them out.

As I wished them well, they turned their attention back to the field. At precisely that moment, the grandson of Roberto Clemente, one of my favorite players as a child, was running the bases to honor his grandfather and all Roberto Clemente Award winners (for community service). On the center-field screen at Safeco Field, the grandson's image, as he circled the bases, was set over that of Roberto Clemente.

Many people began to tear up. I was one. And maybe I wasn't alone putting picture upon picture upon picture.

I saw a twelve-year-old boy who cannot walk smile for a young boy running to honor his grandfather. And I saw Mark Sansaver running against Terese Rehfeldt. I saw ghost runners when once we didn't need them.

Wiffle L.A.

Every serious Wiffle ball player thinks his backyard stadium is unique to the sport. And that's the way it should be, just as everyone's baby is the cutest in the world (except for those born to honest parents).

We go to great lengths to put up the grandest Wiffle ball stadia. In my case, my father (see "Wiffle Ball") built an outfield fence, replete with advertising.

But no man I know has gone to more expense to construct a Wiffle field as extraordinary as that in the hills above Los Angeles. It is there where Rick Messina bought the house next door to his *to expand his Wiffle ball field.*

He has also spent a bunch of his money frivolously.

Messina is the manager for both Tim Allen and Drew Carey, which is to say he prints money for a living.

Hollywood Exec: Rick, I have another project for either Tim or
    Drew: a remake of anything. It pays twenty-five mil.
Rick: We'll take it.

With his workday done, Rick Messina can then go about (a) ordering a fifteenth television monitor for his rec room, so those who aren't in the Wiffle ball game can see another angle of the action; (b) considering the purchase of the other house next door, just because; or (c) considering the purchase of the Goodyear blimp so as to capture overhead shots of the games in play.

The only knock on Messina's stadium is that the field is made of a sport-court surface. Behind the batter is a very large sheet of aluminum, *the* strike zone. If a ball hits the aluminum, it's a strike. Otherwise, standard "line" rules of Wiffle ball apply. That is, one mark for a single, a bobbled grounder an error, one or more bounces to the wall, a double, and off the wall in the air, a triple. Home runs hit *actual seats from Yankee Stadium.* (No, Matt McGillen didn't steal them.)

There's also a Juggs gun, to measure the speed of the pitch.

Messina's home has many bedrooms, a dining room, a living room, and an office. There's a swimming pool in the backyard. But never in my half dozen visits there have I seen anyone spend one minute in one square inch of any area except the rec room (to watch Wiffle ball and other sports), the kitchen (but only to grab a beer), and the Wiffle ball stadium. Why there's a kitchen at all when the garage that adjoins the stadium has a fully stocked refrigerator is anyone's guess.

I've never heard Rick say what the name of the stadium is.

Money would be a good name.

But he could have done other things with his money. He could have purchased cars (he has just one) or boats (none). No. He put his money into the game we love. The second-greatest game to tackle football, and everyone knows this.

If the neighbors on the other side of Messina (from the empty house he bought to expand his field) ever complain about the midnight games, the loud pinging of Wiffle balls making strike noise, or the loud celebrations and arguments, then those people don't understand what's at stake. For all they know, Gary Shandling is down 0-2 in the count, waiting for *the* pitch to drive into the seats, Rick is on a lawn chair smoking a cigar, and a half dozen others are inside the rec room, one eye on Wiffle to see when it's their turn and one eye on *Monday Night Football.* If those neighbors don't like it, they'll never understand what it meant for Mark Sansaver to hit number 715 in 1972, for Matt McGillen to acquire a stop sign that helped make the games at Alma competitive. If they don't get it, they don't get it. It's not our problem. But if they complain, there's a sign they will understand: Just Sold. Rick Messina may want a place for relief pitchers to get warm.

A fact.

From 1956 until 1992 the familiar Wiffle ball box displayed a picture and endorsement from a big-league star such as Whitey Ford, Ted Williams, or Pete Rose. I don't know what happened after that but I'll look next time I'm at a store that sells Wiffle ball equipment. When I was just starting in TV in Seattle, I once asked former Mariners manager Dick Williams, "So, is it just me or have you had trouble purchasing Wiffle ball equipment this spring?" He told me it wasn't funny.

Two-Minute Warning

Two-minute warning." It sounds so ominous. Some other tackle football terms are that way too. "The bomb," for instance. That was the olden-time expression for going deep. Going deep is just one among many terms meaning the same thing for the tackle football pass route drawn below.

Going Deep

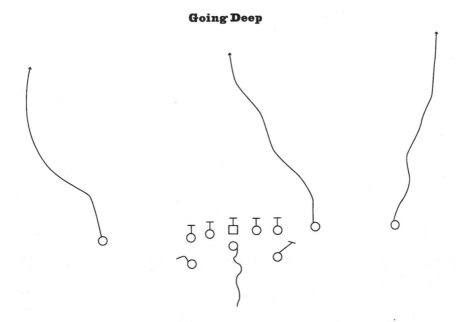

The route, often misnamed "pattern," the pattern actually being a concert of various routes run by various tackle football men, has several other names:

Go
Fly
House
Deep
Long

There may be others, but even if so, they are often the last best choice to run once the *two-minute warning* has been given. If Team A leads Team B by six points with two minutes remaining, and Team B has the ball at the time of the *warning,* Team A will often move into a "prevent defense." The prevent defense is meant to *prevent* bad things from happening to the defense, such as touchdowns. Team A's defensive backs line up in a softer coverage setup, backing way off the line of scrimmage. Team B then passes the ball underneath the coverage and moves the ball easily up the field, a circumstance Team A is earnestly trying to prevent, hence the name "prevent defense."

I often wonder, as I watch Team B move effortlessly down the field, why, if Team A's non*prevent defense* was working well enough to secure a six-point lead, it didn't just stick with what had been successful so far.

Other people wonder this too. The one whose wonder matters most, because he has the right to yell at people, especially the players who aren't even as good as those playing *prevent,* the ones giving up all that yardage, is the head coach of Team A. He is wondering why his defensive coordinator is such an idiot.

There are now thirty-four seconds to go, and Team B is within striking distance to score a touchdown, add an extra point, and win the game. Team A could have used a *one-minute warning.* That might have alerted the guys to the fact that the *prevent defense* may end up preventing Team A from winning. At this point, the head coach is yelling at people, the defensive coordinator has called off the *prevent defense,* and a man in a striped shirt is happy that in thirty-four seconds he gets to fire a gun.

Team B scores a touchdown on the next play, adds the extra point, squib kicks the ball to *prevent* a big return, and hands Team A the ball at its 40-yard line.

There are now twenty-six seconds to play, so Team B goes into its own *prevent defense* so as not to give up *the bomb,* but Team B forgets that Team A doesn't even want a touchdown at this point. Team A needs only a three-point field goal to have its name listed above Team B's name in the paper the next day.

With nineteen seconds remaining Team A has the ball on Team B's 35-yard line. Two passes fall incomplete, not because Team B was *preventing* anything, but because a receiver who'll be cut on Monday dropped the ball twice.

At this point there are five seconds to go before the man fires the gun. A tackle football player with a foreign-sounding name jogs onto the field to kick a 52-yard field goal for the win. In olden times it would have been a 42-yard field goal. That was when the goalposts were located on the goal line. At some point, maybe the point when league officials started to become concerned about all the players who kept running into the goalposts on the goal line, the goalposts were moved to the end line, adding 10 yards of kicking distance for all the foreign-sounding players.

In Canada, where there is a lot of undeveloped land, the end zones are the size of an aircraft carrier. I haven't been to a CFL game in years and don't really remember where those people station their goalposts, or if they even have any. I'm on an airplane right now and there is no Internet access. Even if there were Internet access, I wouldn't take the time to look it up. It doesn't matter right now. What matters is the underlying theme of this chapter. What is this chapter about, anyway? I've lost my train of thought. I just took off my seat belt while the warning sign to wear a seat belt is on. I'm wild. I had a point to make about something and I don't know what it is.

Two-minute warning.

That wasn't the point. That was just the name of the chapter. Oh, I know. It's that people, whether they are tackle football players or not, shouldn't alter whatever it is they do well just because some other people try to put pressure on them. Just because the guy you work with gets red in the face and acts like he's working hard when there's a crisis, real or imagined, doesn't mean he's a good worker. It just means he gets red in the face. He'd be a terrible guy to have as your quarterback when the *two-minute warning* is given. Get rid of him. He sucks.

I don't know if Team A made the field goal or not. There are no teams in the NFL called Team A and Team B. Why are we spending so much valuable book space on these fictitious teams?

This here is way more important.

As I said, I'm on an airplane. I barely made my flight. I left for Los Angeles International in my rental car with plenty of time to spare. Then I found out the lame rental car company I was set up with *closes its rental office at 10 p.m.* Who closes its rental car office at 10 p.m.? Enterprise Rental Car, that's who.

You're telling me the second-most-populous city in America has a rental car company that closes down at 10 p.m.? Actually, I don't know for sure if L.A. is the second most populous city. Las Vegas is getting pretty big lately. I'm not going to look it up. I can't. I'm on an airplane. I guess I could ask somebody. But then I'd look stupid. But I look stupid anyway, so I should just ask. But everyone around me is asleep. The lady across from me is wearing those large felt eye covers. What the hell is she, a racehorse? Is she pretending she's a hostage and her captors don't want her to know the location of their secret hideout? Is she making a statement that she doesn't want to be bothered with inane airplane chatter?

Passenger #1: Headed home?
Passenger #2: No. I have a couple days of business in [insert city].
Passenger #1: Yeah. Yeah. I had a four-hour layover in Chicago. Sheesh. Air travel. Can't live with it. Can't live without women.

Passenger #2: And the food. Don't get me started.
Passenger #1: It's not like the old days. Back when Kenny
  Mayne's dad used a green felt-tip pen to move everyone up
  to first class.
Passenger #2: That was a great chapter.

The lady with the horse blinkers just took them off, got up, and went to the restroom. I'm going to ask her where Los Angeles ranks in terms of the nation's most populous cities when she gets back to her seat. Then I'm going to make her proofread this book.

So I'm driving down La Cienega on the way to the rental car place. This place was chosen by the folks at *Dancing with the Stars* (whom I worked for today) because making twenty million per show just isn't enough. No, they have to use a discount rental car place to jack up the profits just a little more. Now I know how Enterprise is able to give better rates than most of the other rental car companies. *BECAUSE ENTERPRISE DOESN'T HAVE TO PAY ITS PEOPLE PAST TEN O'CLOCK AT NIGHT.*

I called ahead to Enterprise, just to make sure I had the directions down correctly. The lady who answered gave me all sorts of complicated turns, slight turns, U-turns. I think she told me to put the car in reverse at one point in the directions. Then she told me she was going to be closing in *one minute.* It was 9:59 p.m.

I asked her how it was the office could be closing at ten o'clock when Los Angeles is the largest city in the world. The lady from Enterprise told me Los Angeles isn't even as big as Rio, and her office was now closed.

The lady with the horse blinkers just got back to her seat. She has blinkers on and she's pretending to be asleep again.

The lady at the car place told me I have to drive twenty miles away and drop the car at some hotel. I told her I would sooner fly the car to the moon than do that. I told her my name is not even on the credit card paying for the car so I will put the car *somewhere.* I need to make my flight more than I need to get a receipt for a rental car I am not paying for.

She told me, "Okay, sir. But if the car is stolen, it's your responsibility."

That's when I told her it would more likely be *Dancing with the Stars'* responsibility. Then I told her I thought Stacy Keibler got screwed, but not as much as me.

Little did the Enterprise rental lady know that not only would the car end up in some airport parking lot but that there might be a problem with the parking brake. Or the transmission. Earlier this morning, it seemed the valet guys at the hotel jammed the parking brake down so hard I couldn't get it to release. I drove across Los Angeles looking like Cheech and Chong. I thought the car was going to catch fire at one point. I called the *Dancing with the Stars* producer to ask if I should pull over and get a cab the rest of the way. The British guy at the other end of the line said the British version of "The show must go on." Then he said, "Brilliant."

It turns out I was wrong about the valet guys. This wasn't one of those cars where you just tap on the foot brake again to release it. This car had an actual *brake release* handle.

The car smoke dissipated. It never did catch fire.

Now it is abandoned. You can have one of your friends steal it tonight if you are on my plane looking over my shoulder.

The car is in some parking lot about four blocks from LAX. I called the dance people to tell them what I did, that it might cost them another fifty dollars to pay for the pickup. Then I called the rental office only to find out not only do they close at 10 p.m. in the fifth-largest city in California, but they don't take messages after hours.

I am running low on battery power.

My computer just gave me a *two-minute warning*.

I'm going into *prevent*.

Time to protect what I have. I am not giving up anything I've gained.

Hail Mary

This sounds like another tackle football chapter but it's really more about a last-ditch effort to get one more thing in the book.

The year: 1989.

The place: Seattle Science Center, Seattle, Washington.

I was with Ken Griffey Jr. in his rookie season. Harold Reynolds (the Mariners' All-Star and Gold Glove second baseman) was there as well.

Griffey had received a lot of attention. He was having a big rookie season.

A large group of Japanese tourists walked up to us. One of them, in broken English, asked Griffey if he would take a picture. Griffey said he would, and walked over to the group.

Then a lady in the group handed him a camera.

They wanted him to *take a picture.*

I saw Griffey at the Major League All-Star event in San Francisco in July of 2007. I hadn't seen him in some time. I was glad he was having such a big year for the Reds.

I asked Griffey if he remembered the day we went to the Seattle Science Center, and he said yes.

Then I told him I was writing a book and that I wanted to include a short note about one of my career highlights. I *outthrew* Ken Griffey Jr. at the Seattle Science Center in a Wiffle ball speed pitch: 63 to 62 miles per hour, if I recall the Wiffle numbers.

Junior: Do you have the video?
Me: I still do.

Junior: But will the book come with the video?
Me: No. Of course not.
Junior: Then I won't back it up.

Then I asked him to take a picture.

Otis, my friend from Seattle, was with me at the All-Star event.

I may have been violating some kind of media rule about not bothering the players for autographs or pictures. But I didn't *take* the picture. Otis did. I just stood there. Right next to a Hall of Famer-to-be. He'll have that one day. I'll have what I have.

If something is true, one needs no confirmation.

Here is a relevant sports fact.

In 1989, I outthrew Ken Griffey Jr. in a Wiffle ball pitch-speed game at the Seattle Science Center.

Yachting

Yachting has a rule book called *The Deed of Gift.* I don't know what it says in there but I'm told it is very complicated.

In yachting, extremely rich people get other people to sail their boats. It is called "America's Cup." Rich American people hate it when rich non-American people win America's Cup, in the same way rich Bulgarian people probably hate it when rich non-Bulgarian people win Powerball, especially when the rich Bulgarian people couldn't get to 7-Eleven on time.

That's yachting as I know it.

I do know about *boats*.

When my son Connor was in the hospital, my wife, Laura, and I would talk about how one day he'd be able to start talking. When he did, we imagined, he'd open with some of those simple one-syllable words, "boat" being our favorite.

"Boat!" became something of a family- and close-friends-only inside tribute to Connor. "Boat!" could be uttered at any time, with any meaning. But mostly, it was a word to bring cheer, particularly in that Connor never had his shot to say "Boat!"

Boat!

My first boat was a four-foot-long blue plastic craft given to me by my father as a get-well present after I had to have a tooth extracted. I was five years old. I thought I was a badass, rowing around that blue four-foot-long plastic boat on Star Lake. For you other five-year-olds about to have a tooth extracted, let me point out that I did wear an orange life vest for safety.

My dad used to give us presents when we were sick. If he heard one of us had stayed home from school, he'd show up after work with some kind of kid toy, something to cheer. I think my sister Carolee missed two years of K–12 schooling.

Boat!

My dad was onto something with that four-foot-long blue plastic boat. Years later, when he saw my son in the hospital in Maine for the first time, he looked at Connor, who weighed in at about two pounds that day, and Dad said, "Maybe he can be a jockey."

That was my dad. Looking to the positive. Looking at things in a way that suggested tomorrow would be a better day than today.

Sure, my tooth had been extracted. But I'll be damned if I wasn't the happiest kid on Star Lake. I had a four-foot-long blue plastic boat. I couldn't have cared less about America's Cup or how the Bulgarians felt about Powerball or 7-Elevens. I owned that lake.

And Connor would have owned any body of water.

Boat.

Boat!

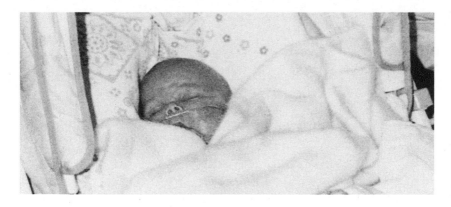

Connor

My dad

Appendix A

A Chapter I Forgot to Write: Name That Seattle Pilot

As you've read, this book contained a lot of childhood memories. I must have been blocking out part of my childhood (and it was a pretty easy childhood) because until my final edit meeting I'd neglected to write about a key summer of my life.

I was nine. It was 1969. America was about to land on the moon. Seattle had landed the Pilots.

They had a theme song that went, "Go, go, you Pilots."

They were going places all right. They went to last place. And then they just up and went.

The former site of their second-rate field is now a home-improvement store.

Seattle Sicks' stadium really did need a fresh coat of paint. That home-improvement store should have come along sooner.

What did I care? I was there in person to watch major league baseball.

My sister Leslie and her boyfriend, Steve McCully, used to let me tag along on their dates. We'd stop at McDonalds. We'd buy cheap outfield seats. We'd watch the Pilots lose.

Partly from that season came Jim Bouton's famous tell-all book, *Ball Four*. At least somebody profited. The team went under. The next spring the players reported to training camp in Arizona as Seattle Pilots. At the end of training the players and equipment were shipped east. Ladies and gentlemen: your Milwaukee Brewers.

It would be seven more years until Seattle got a baseball team. Kids like me shifted our loyalties and supported teams from elsewhere. Most of the guys went down the coast and backed San Francisco or

Los Angeles. I jumped on the Cincinnati Reds. They were title winners in those years, so the loss of the Pilots didn't sting as much.

The Pilots are mostly forgotten. In fact, as I know it, there are only two others on earth who can stay with me in a game of Name That Pilot. (You have thirty seconds to name the next Pilot or you're out.) They are Jerry Hanley, my old friend and photographer, and Steve Vecchione, a senior producer at ESPN. Vech and I haven't had a real conversation in years. Each time we see each other in the hall, one of us says something like "Tommy Harper" (he led the AL in stolen bases in 1969 with 73), and then the other says "Jim Bouton."

"Don Mincher."

"Gus Gil."

"Jerry McNertney."

"Steve Hovely."

Jerry and Vech aren't here, but I can go longer.

"Marty Pattin."

"Wayne Comer."

"Diego Segui" (started the franchise opener both for the Pilots and the Mariners).

"Fred Talbot" (who once hit a grand slam to win a $25,000 radio contest).

"Tommy Davis." (We should have kept him.)

I'm sorry. I have to stop. It's not that it's so painful. It's just that neither Jerry nor Vech are here and season opener for *The Wire* just came on. The Pilots won't mind. Just knowing that there are three of us left who can play Name That Pilot ought to count for something.

"Gene Brabender."

"Joe Shultz" (manager).

"Sal Maglie" (pitching coach).

"Ray Oyler."

"Mike Hegan."

> **True fact: Boog Powell once hit an inside-the-park home run against the Seattle Pilots.**

Appendix B

Other Books I Might Write

This is the part in a book where you're supposed to be able to see how I researched a bunch of stuff in scholarly fashion. At this point, what does it matter if any of the preceding was true? It's already been written. The time for checking facts was way back before those people at the book company hit the Go button and started printing this thing. It's too late now. All there's left to do is list a bunch of other books I might or might not write. Mostly, I've just written a bunch of e-mails.

1. ***The Complete and Accurate History of My E-mails.*** My agent told me if this book sells at all, we can sell another one right quick to a whole bunch of publishers because they're all greedy bastards and would see the success of this book and then start counting up the dollars to be made by having me type up anything. Even *The Complete and Accurate History of My E-mails.* At this point, I'm really liking this whole author thing. I've daydreamed about showing up on the *Today* show, bantering and giggling with Katie Couric, and having her touch my arm just before commercial break in a way that says, "Come back anytime, author." That was a stupid daydream to have because she doesn't even work at the *Today* show any longer. Plus, in that I'm part of the Disney family, I shouldn't be having illicit dreams about any morning shows except *Good Morning America* on ABC. I like that show and everything, but no one on it ever gets to say, "But first, this is *Today* on NBC." I love it when people say that, and I thought after bantering and giggling with Katie, maybe they'd let me do that. Anyway, this book will be

about all my e-mails, which recipients will tell you are among the best. I could do a short book on out-of-office replies because my out-of-office replies are just plain good, I'm telling you. My agent told me the greedy people in the publishing world will print anything for a second book if the first book sold more than expected. My agent is pretty greedy too, so I don't know if I want to be a part of this project. Plus, I have no idea how to find all my sent e-mails at this point. Anyway, that book is well on its way.

2. ***Kenny Mayne Takes Out the Trash.***   You're probably thinking this is going to be like *A Current Affair,* or one of those other Journalism with a capital J exposé shows. But instead, it's just about taking out the trash. I used to be a garbageman, as noted, and for some reason, maybe to keep it real (how real can you keep it in Connecticut?) I like to take my own trash to the garbage dump. I think it might be because my dad used to take our trash to the dump himself, though not all the time. I mean, we did have the weekly garbagemen visit. I had to drag three metal garbage cans up our long and scary driveway, sometimes in the dark. But on those occasions when we'd had a big party or maybe after Christmas, with all that Christmas stuff, my dad would load up the car, drive to the dump, pay a fee, and then let me throw stuff into the giant container. This may have been what made me semidestructive. I loved to break glass, watch electronic equipment explode, and hurl spoiled fruit into the giant metal container. Back in those days there was no such thing as recycling. Most people threw garbage out their car windows. Not us. My parents threw only lit cigarettes out the window. Unlike my father, I don't drive to the dump once in a while with the extra garbage on those heavy-garbage times during the year. Instead, I pay seventy-five dollars for the yearly pass and take my own garbage once a week or more. What is wrong with me? Anyway, this should be quite a book. It'll be a bit like that Al Gore global-warming book, but mostly it will be about how I still get to break stuff, though now I break the bottles in the appropriate place, the recycling area. There might be a chapter also about how my wife and I often give away things our family no longer needs. I drop that

off in the Community Share area at the transfer station, then watch women get out of Volvos and Mercedeses to fight it out over our unwanted lamps. This book needs a lot of work but at least I know there'll be tons more garbage, whereas in that first extra book of mine, the one about e-mails, it's anyone's guess if the material is going to be available.

3. ***Kenny Mayne's Grocery List.*** You, like me, have no doubt looked at a Jackson Pollock painting, hanging in a museum, or sitting against a lamp at a Community Share area, and thought, "I could do that." But, if you, like me, ever really tried to paint like Jackson Pollock, you ended up thinking, "How come his paintings didn't all end up looking like the December turf at the old Cleveland Browns' Municipal Stadium, where they spray-painted the mud green so TV viewers would think it was grass?" Grocery lists as art, that's what that book will probably be about. That's unless I get a quarter of the way through it and come up with a better idea. I won't really make this my third book. This definitely sounds like a second book. Those are supposed to be terrible, just a vehicle to pile up some money after the success of the breakthrough work. You publishing bastards think we don't have you figured out? We can read you like a . . . book.

4. ***Why Gene Hickerson Should Be in the Hall of Fame.*** This idea actually came from my agent. I don't even know who Gene Hickerson is. In fact, I know so little about Gene Hickerson, I don't know which Hall of Fame he should be in. This reminds me of the time period (my blue period) when I was doing a lot of freelance television work. Most of it was for ESPN, but sometimes I would pick up a day of work with a TV station from the town whose NFL team was playing the Seahawks that week. I would call all the TV stations in the opposing town and ask if they were sending a crew for the game against the Seahawks. Once in a while, the smaller stations would jump at the idea and hire me for a fraction of what it would have cost to send a full staff to get the terribly necessary postgame interviews for the big clash that Sunday with the Seattle Seahawks. The Seahawks staff knew me, and I'd get press passes for me and my

cameraman, Rob Weller. After the game, however, I would come to realize that I didn't really know very many of the players by face, other than a few of the team's stars. Usually the stars go into the training room after the game and put ice on their injured parts or, worse still, put clothes on their naked bodies and leave. That would leave me and my cameraman with no one but semianonymous tackle football players from a town that had a TV station willing to pay me money to interview people involved in a big clash with the Seahawks. Knowing that I had to talk with somebody to have really worked for the station paying me all that money, I would go up to the naked players and start asking questions about the big game that had just occurred. Having been trained halfway well in journalism, I used all my investigative skills to, if nothing else, identify the player I was talking with. The line of questioning went something like, "So, big guy, that was some game." I would leave out the rest of what I was really trying to ask, such as "Some game played by you *if* indeed you played in the game." By continuing to ask very probing questions and by trying to look at the number on the naked man's jersey, which was rolled up inside a mesh bag near his locker, I would ascertain which side of the ball this man played on and then start zeroing in on exactly what it was he did for a living. This was a far better, and far less embarrassing, approach than asking, "So, big guy, what's going through your mind right now as either a defensive or offensive player who either did or didn't play and either had or didn't have much of an impact on the big clash that just occurred on the gridiron? Congratulations, I think."

So this is how I feel right now about whatever that guy's name is my agent wants me to write a book about. My agent grew up near Cleveland and he may also have had something to do with that Pollock reference to Cleveland's Municipal Stadium. Why the hell didn't my agent just write a book? I hadn't really intended to get all mushy here at the end, but it is true that without my agent, whatever his name is, I probably wouldn't have written my book and for certain I wouldn't have written this other proposed book. I was just sitting around doing television stuff and being a husband and father and betting on horses whenever possible. That was really enough for me. But then he told me I should write a book. Not this stupid proposed book that will never get off the ground, but that other book, the one you just read. So I did it. And now I'm done and he cannot make me write another one especially about some guy I've never heard of. But if I took my time, and tried very hard, I bet I could make a compelling case for the guy to be in the Hall of Fame. As it turns out, I just glanced down at my agent's notes with regard to this ending bit, an "appendix," they call it. It turns out that guy *did* make it to the Hall of Fame. When I decided to become an author, I was never so vain to think I'd have that kind of an impact on society. I just like to write. For that, screw the agent, I give all the credit to my mother. That's how you end a book. Even if it's just an appendix, whatever that is. Please put the book back in the correct place on the shelf in case somebody actually buys it. We need to sell as many as possible to stand a chance at getting to write a second book.

The end.

Appendix C

Modern Art

Riley and Annie wanted to prove they are better artists now than when I gave them a false deadline in May 2007. Here they are drawing each other in February 2008.

Acknowledgments

No one helped very much.

Even More Acknowledgments

Okay, my editor, Sean Desmond, helped a little. And Shawn Nicholls did a nice job on the Web site. The few facts we went with, my friend Todd Snyder made sure they were right. And my agent and wife were given lots of praise earlier, deservedly so.

Index of People Not Mentioned in the Book